L.

22

A LONG WAY FROM MISSOURI

Also by Mary Margaret McBride:

HARVEST OF AMERICAN COOKING

TUNE IN FOR ELIZABETH

HOW DEAR TO MY HEART

A LONG WAY
FROM MISSOURI

Mary Margaret McBride

G. P. Putnam's Sons
New York

B
M

© 1959 BY MARY MARGARET McBRIDE

Library of Congress Catalog
Card Number: 59-6172

Second Impression

MANUFACTURED IN THE UNITED STATES OF AMERICA

Contents

A LONG WAY FROM MISSOURI

1. Young Woman Goes East

"TERRIBLE things happen to young girls in New York City," my mother reflected dubiously.

"Bosh," scoffed my father. "Sister is big enough to take care of herself. And Aunt Alsandra will see that she behaves."

I took care not to remind my parents that though Aunt Alsandra lived in New York State, she was more than 200 miles removed from Manhattan and had been there only once in 40 years, after which she vowed that she'd never set foot in the place again.

"It's dirty and noisy and the people aren't even civil," my great-aunt had mentioned bitterly to me. I remember the occasion well because the very next night our spare-room bed collapsed under her 250 pounds.

Aunt Alsandra's attitude didn't affect my own in the least. Ever since I was five years old I'd been determined to go to New York and get on a newspaper. Even as I listened to my father and mother debate the point, I knew very well that it made no difference what they said: the time had come for me to go to New York and get on a newspaper. There was even more to my ambition: I intended after an apprenticeship on a newspaper to become a great novelist and so rich that I could take my mother on a trip to Europe.

My two grandfathers (Grandpa McBride who taught me Greek and Latin poetry and Grandpa Bee Craig, a Baptist preacher who told me stories) agreed that I would certainly be a great writer and I firmly believed them. We had it all planned out that first I would be a reporter and from that I would go on to CREATE novels.

The reason we were discussing my going to New York was that after two years and a half of summer schools and regular sessions, I'd emerged from the University of Missouri School of Journalism with a Bachelor of Journalism degree, the credits for which were received partly by work on a town daily and partly by the indulgent attitude of the faculty who gave me better grades than I deserved— largely, I think, because they were tired of seeing me struggle to keep my eyes open in class after a hard night on the paper.

"I've never known anyone to go so far on sympathy,"

Novelist Faith Baldwin told me years later. I suspect she may be right, for though I've always meant to be staunch and courageous, the truth is that I cry too easily, often feel sorry for myself and take advantage of kindness.

As it turned out, my mother saw me off for the East, almost without tears because she was relieved that my first destination was to be the Nation's Capital (east all right but not wicked New York) where she knew I would find waiting a responsible and concerned guardian in the person of a family friend, middle-aged Douglas Meng, Missouri newspaperman who had become Assistant Sergeant at Arms of the U. S. Senate.

Douglas—naturally I called him Mr. Meng—sent for me because he planned to start a Washington news service for small Missouri papers and felt I might help him gather items.

You wouldn't have known it to look at me—I was still wearing a middy blouse, pleated skirt to my lisle-stockinged ankles and a spit curl in the middle of my forehead —but I was definitely a young woman WITH A PURPOSE. Most girls that I knew were determined to have careers. Marriage was all right, we thought—but for later. First had to come the job. I had absolutely no social consciousness—not even a great concern about women and the vote. I was just engrossed in myself and my ambitions. At least some of my companions in journalism school were the same.

I remember one day in chemistry lab a classmate named Julia and me being sunk in gloom because the first world war was ending without us. We were convinced that we would never amount to anything because we hadn't been female Richard Harding Davises, right up in the front lines.

This kind of determination was something fairly new for the Middle Western female. At least I was the first woman in my family who had ever aspired to be anything but a teacher or at any rate dreamed that she could be. But the very fact that I'd worked my way through college on that paper instead of waiting on tables or washing dishes showed that I was part of a new era. I knew all about pioneers in the field I hoped to enter—Dorothy Dix and Winifred Black, front-page sob sisters—but not much about that group of dedicated crusaders, Jane Addams, Carrie Chapman Catt and the rest who were making a new world for all women.

The trip to Washington was real adventure. I had never been out of Missouri before in my life and naturally had never slept on a train. I had Upper 12 and an unknown man had Lower 12. I was terrified of climbing to the top berth. I was nervous about the man and wouldn't ask the porter anything because I didn't want him to guess how little I knew. I couldn't figure out how to put on the light so I just stuck my shoes and hat in the little hammock in the darkness. I didn't undress, I didn't go into the dining car (luckily my mother had put part of a fried chicken and some buttered biscuits in my satchel) and it took all my courage finally to creep desperately to the dressing room.

I carried a few dollars (left over from an aunt's gift) carefully arranged in the grosgrain band of my round childish beaver hat. My strong distrust of banks was inherited from my father, I guess. Anyway, it stayed with me for years. I never had a purse in those days and my handkerchief and powder rag were tucked down my front.

Mr. Meng, perspiring copiously and mopping vigorously—he weighed 300 pounds and had three chins—met me at Union Station and carried my imitation leather valise to a taxicab which took us to the unfashionable northeast section where he had rented for me a hall bedroom in the apartment of a druggist and his wife. Even the modest $5-a-week rent the druggist asked was more than I could afford, but I optimistically paid up the first seven days in advance. The druggist's wife could give me toast and coffee for breakfast. Other meals would be eaten out.

My room had in it a brass double bed, a rickety veneered dresser, a buckling and clouded mirror. A washstand held a flowered bowl and pitcher. The room, however, was spotless, the curtains crisp, and I didn't mind at all sharing with the family the bathroom at the end of the hall. Bathrooms still seemed pretty wonderful to my country eyes.

My landlady was a plump, fresh-faced woman with kind blue eyes. I liked her at once and wrote my mother a reassuring note about my surroundings.

The very next day I went to work at the Capitol. The news service project was only a mimeograph machine with stencils at this juncture (it never got much beyond that) and since I had to live, Douglas put me on the payroll of a Missouri senator who happened to have a post free. When the solon soon had to bestow this political plum on the daughter of an important constituent, I was transferred to some other senator with a vacancy, and so on and on. The result was that every paycheck was a surprise— sometimes good, sometimes bad.

In the few months I was around the Capitol I must have been employed by half a dozen senators—sometimes for only two weeks at a time—and all I'm sure of is that I seldom made more than $20 a week ($10 more than I got for covering the courthouse and related beats back in Columbia, Missouri) .

I never did discover the exact duties of a "folder"— this was my official designation in the office of the Sergeant at Arms. My chores consisted mostly of making out gasoline vouchers for senators who filled their automobile tanks at cost. In addition I rose respectfully when a senator entered the office and handed him a glass of ice water. Once in a while, as necessary, I typed a voucher for the funeral of some deceased legislator (I remember that cigars, cigarettes, mineral water and sometimes stronger liquids were among the items) .

I was very well satisfied with my unexciting life until the whirlwind arrival of my rich Kansas City cousin Gladys, accompanied by four trunks.

MEET ME AT 4:35 AT UNION STATION. I'M GOING TO GET A JOB TOO, her lengthy telegram informed me. Sure enough, she did get one right away, a clerkship in the Navy Department. Anything less likely than my glamorous young cousin filing dull reports in dusty cabinets I couldn't imagine, but she loved the only real work she'd ever done in all her sheltered life.

After her first three days with me, the druggist's wife asked embarrassedly, "Does your cousin intend to stay?" When I, equally embarrassed, stammered that I didn't know, she suggested that maybe we'd find roomier quarters elsewhere since the hall was rather cluttered with Gladys's trunks and the room was chaos, for Gladys was even more untidy than I.

My cousin took the news of our eviction in good humor and said she already had her eye on an apartment in a swankier section of Washington. When I protested that I

16

couldn't afford it, she reassured me firmly. "That's all right. I'll pay for it. I need somebody to live with me and we'll have fun together."

We did have fun, too, including that very day when Gladys bought an Oakland coupé from an automobile showroom and drove away in it, though she knew as little as I did about how to handle a car. We wobbled off, and luckily policemen were friendly to a pretty young woman with winning ways and so, though we were oftener on the left side of the road than the right and had two dented fenders and a bent radiator by the end of the first week, we survived and went on gaily driving around Washington.

We finally settled that I would pay what I'd been paying for the hall bedroom, and moved into the swanky apartment. Gladys immediately installed Sophie as cook, a wonderful hand with pastries, custards, whipped cream cakes and every other kind of rich dessert. Almost at once I knew that Sophie would be my undoing, but I had no wish to curb her art.

My generous cousin further complicated my weight problem by lavish gifts of boxes of my favorite chocolate caramels—bribes, mostly, to keep me from nagging her about anything I disapproved of. I could be very unpleasant but not when eating caramels. I often think I might have been quite a different shape if it hadn't been for those few months in Washington.

Life was not all luscious meals in our new apartment, though. After a few nights, I was covered with red splotches which itched unbearably and soon I discovered that the blemishes were occasioned by little hard-shelled crawling creatures. Sophie identified them as bedbugs and my shocked cousin removed us to the Willard Hotel while exterminators sealed up the apartment and burned lethal candles. When they said it was safe, we moved back —though the rooms still smelled of chemicals.

I went trustingly to sleep that night. But next morning I woke up all over splotches. Further investigation revealed that the bugs were in the old walls to stay. So we moved again, this time to a more recently built, quite modern-looking apartment.

Maybe you won't believe it, but it's the truth: my old enemies were there, too. For some reason they never bit Gladys, so I had to show her samples not only of bites but bugs. This time she called in not just exterminators but a mattress shop, and between them they managed to get rid of the intruders.

Until Gladys got a brand-new telephone number, however, we were afflicted with another type of annoyance. The apartment, we found, had been occupied by what Gladys and I referred to as a lady of the evening. Gladys made a funny story of it when dining out, but I felt it was all disgraceful.

There were plenty of chances to tell the story, for Gladys knew an incredible number of important people, and wherever she was invited she insisted on dragging me. When I complained that I had nothing to wear, she promptly presented me with half a dozen of her own almost new dresses which, in spite of my inroads on Sophie's cooking, fitted me perfectly.

There was a lot of lavish Washington entertaining in those days. I remember especially the buffets which included great hams and turkeys and all kinds of delicious cream cakes—layer after layer—and things called "shapes" which were gelatin and Bavarian cream desserts in the form of flowers. I felt sorry for some of the little old ladies who turned up regularly at these parties—widows, I was told, of once important Washington men who had stayed on in the city, living on tiny pensions. The parties helped supplement their slender means and many a time I saw one skinny gray-haired wisp dressed in the fashion of the nineties surreptitiously slipping a few sandwiches or some ham or cake into her oversized handbag.

I wore Gladys's clothes to parties, but I was still appearing at the office of the Sergeant at Arms in my favorite middies and skirts. Some senator (or senators) decided this attire was too informal for a folder in such a distinguished office. And to poor Douglas Meng fell the unhappy task of telling me. Doug had the kindest heart in the world. Perspiration rolled down his distressed face and his eyes refused to meet mine as he blurted out the Senate dictum that I'd have to give up either middy blouses or my job. Luckily, by that time I was fretting about how I would ever get on a newspaper if I stayed in the Senate office building and didn't mind too much. Then the situation solved itself: a telegram came from a schoolmate—Pauline Pfeiffer, later the second Mrs. Ernest Hemingway—telling me that she had persuaded her editor to try me out at $35 a week on the Cleveland *Press*. She had been working on the *Press* ever since graduation.

I was certain the $35 was a typographical error. Certainly they wouldn't pay more than $25, I thought, but I took the telegram with me as evidence and left next morning for Cleveland. Gladys was upset, but by that time she was a little bored with her job, and besides, her family wanted her to go back home.

He was too considerate to say so, of course, but I'm sure Douglas was relieved, for he had undoubtedly had a tough time keeping me supplied with Senate paychecks. Cleveland still seemed east to me though really I suppose I was retracing my steps a little. But that didn't matter: while Washington was nearer, Cleveland was a mere overnight train trip to New York.

Cleveland was cold and Pauline wasn't at the station. I took a taxicab to the *Press*, bags and all. (I had two bags now because of Gladys's additions to my wardrobe.) At the paper I found that Pauline had been called home that day by a death in her family. The editor himself would see me, said the office boy. I went in, clutching my telegram with its promise of $35 a week. I didn't need it, for the editor, after greeting me, proceeded to business: "We are paying you $35," he summed up. "It's probably more than any woman reporter is worth. And if you aren't worth it, out you will have to go!"

I think he only wanted the situation to be clear, but his announcement was like a dash of ice water. He sent me on to the city editor, who gave me two assignments, one in Lakewood, one in East Cleveland, the entire length of Cleveland apart. Since I hadn't the least idea how to get round by streetcar, I took taxicabs. That day's journeying cost me $16 and I ended up at the expensive Statler Hotel because I didn't know where else to go.

By that time my funds were so low that I didn't dare eat in the hotel dining room so I went to bed hungry. Next day at the office another reporter told me about a room I could rent and a boardinghouse that would feed me.

Then began at once the severest and most effective training I've ever experienced. The *Press* had an imaginary reader, Mike Zabosky (Cleveland had many foreign-born) and reporters were cautioned to write so clearly and simply that Mike could never misunderstand a word.

As a general reporter for the *Press* I covered everything from murder to markets, learned to concentrate on leads, to be fast and accurate writing a yarn from some other reporter's notes or from a publicity release. I often turned out as many as fourteen pieces of copy in a day.

One of my scariest adventures was taking my first ride in an airplane. Airplane trips were still so unusual for the average layman that the city editor said, "There might be a story in it but you'll have to do it on your own. The paper won't assign you." So I put my name to a legal document that said I went up of my own accord, so that if I got killed the paper couldn't be held. The mischievous pilot did the falling leaf, Immelmann turns and worse, so I was dizzy but relieved when I landed back on earth. I got my story and the *Press* published it with my by-line. A shiver went down my spine a few months later when I read of the death of that pilot in a plane crash.

Another adventure I owed to the *Press* was being credited by a couple who were on the verge of divorce, with saving their marriage. I had been to see the woman about their troubles and she was so broken up she couldn't speak. I decided she must really love her husband. When I finally got her started she talked for two hours, and then I went to see the man. He didn't want a divorce, he confessed, and the two decided to patch up their differences and try again.

My first Christmas away from home was dismal, for my box from the family failed to come, and I spent Christmas Eve in a neighborhood motion picture house looking at a Mary Pickford feature as well as I could through the tears that streamed down my cheeks. Then I went to the corner drugstore and absorbed two chocolate ice cream sodas in rapid succession—still crying, but not quite so much. Years later I told that story on Jack Paar's television program and everybody laughed. I asked comedienne Dody Goodman, sitting next to me, "Did I tell it wrong? Why did they laugh?"

She answered, "No, you told it all right. I think the trouble is, you told it in a mink stole. You'll never get sympathy in a mink stole."

Pauline didn't come back to Cleveland but I made other friends, mostly in the office, and even found time for occasional dates with the business manager of the *Press* and a young man studying at Western Reserve.

The turning point in my life in Cleveland was an interfaith religious convention I was sent to cover. I had been brought up in a very strict Baptist home and was still close enough to my early training to believe that religion was something to treat very reverently. So when the delegates got into what appeared to me an unseemly argument about labor and unions, I skipped that part of the proceedings when I wrote my story.

Next day the city editor stopped at my desk with the opposition papers in his hands. They both headlined the labor skirmishes.

"What reason did you have for not reporting this?" inquired the editor with deceptive gentleness.

"I thought they shouldn't have talked like that at a meeting of a religious organization," I replied earnestly.

Why he didn't fire me that minute I'll never know, but he didn't. Instead, he showed me a letter from a representative of the convention. It said I was the only reporter who had covered the event soberly.

The city editor looked down at me grimly. "If the other

reporters had a drink or two," he advised, with never a smile, "I wish you'd take one next time."

The following day there was a note for me from the interfaith group representative. He offered me a job at the New York City headquarters of the organization for $10 less than I was getting on the *Press*. But it was my chance for New York and though the *Press* dangled a tempting raise, I extravagantly telegraphed my answer: ARRIVE TO-MORROW.

At last I was really on my way. Once I was actually in New York City, that great novel I was going to write would be only a matter of time.

Vasiliu

2. New York, Here I Come

IN MY whole life there never can be anything that even comes near the thrill of that first Saturday in New York. I stepped off the night train from Cleveland into Grand Central Station on one of those crisp, clear, just-cool-enough mornings that delude the newcomer into thinking Manhattan is always like that—never humid, torrid or murky as other places are. In addition to my natural exultation at finally reaching the city of my dreams, I was feeling supremely pleased with myself. This third night on a Pullman except for overtipping a little, I had behaved like a seasoned traveler.

Hortense Saunders, a fellow worker on the Cleveland *Press,* who had been to New York not once but twice, had recommended the Seville Hotel and had even engaged a room for me. And no sooner had I entered it than the telephone rang. Hortense, it seemed, had also arranged a blind date for me, though I doubt I would have recognized it by that description then.

The caller was a Hungarian newspaperman, once a foreign editor of the *Press* and now on a Manhattan daily. Max had a rich, persuasive voice which I later found matched his melting dark eyes. The bit of an accent added to his allure. He invited me to lunch and I hardly had time to unpack before there he was at the desk downstairs, waiting with what he managed to make me feel was eager impatience.

He took me to lunch at an intimate little Hungarian restaurant where the veal paprika and apricot soufflé would have enchanted me if I had not been too diverted by Max's ardent manner to notice food. I can't imagine anything that could provide a finer build-up for a country girl newly come to the big city than a Hungarian stranger who almost instantly becomes a suitor. He left me at my hotel after lunch with obvious reluctance but by that time we already had an engagement for dinner.

As soon as I thought he was out of sight, I rushed back downstairs and out to the street. For three hours I roamed New York. I even located the Woolworth Building and gawked up at it with awe.

Most of the time I had no idea where I was, but once I was horror-stricken to see a street sign that read THE

BOWERY. Quite suddenly, I became almost hysterical with fright. I looked around desperately, perfectly certain that gunmen were pointing their deadly weapons at me, drunks were lurching toward me, criminals were ready to assault me. Visible were only a few shabby-looking men slouching along the street and two cats engaged in an argument over a sardine tin. All the same I fairly ran down a side street and never stopped until the sign said THIRD AVENUE. I didn't know anything about Third Avenue, but at least it wasn't the Bowery.

Back at the Seville a great pasteboard box, almost as big as a coffin, waited for me. Inside, snuggled two dozen —I counted them—deep red American Beauty roses. I hugged them to my bosom, thorns and all, and gazed rapturously at the card which read *For a lovely lady . . .* MAX.

I'd never been called a lovely lady in my life and I had sense enough to know that the title was excessive. But I was blissful anyway.

Dinner continued the magic. The Brevoort Hotel on lower Fifth Avenue offered French cooking and, more than that, a completely Latin atmosphere with small tables, soft rose lighting, young men and women holding hands— even kissing, some of them, right out in public. At Max's assumption that I knew all about such exotic dishes, and even preferred them, I ate snails in garlic-butter sauce that night for the first time. Luckily, Max called them "escargots" so I didn't realize until a good while afterwards what they really were. I also tackled crepes suzette and concealed my astonishment and some alarm as the waiter concocted them right at our table and served them with the sauce still flaming.

I was wearing, because I wanted to dress up for Max,

one of the dresses Gladys had given me—an emerald-green velvet, discreetly ankle length with, for me, a rather tight skirt, and a small toque—also Gladys's gift—of the same velvet. By the time I got to New York I had finally abandoned the curl in the middle of my forehead and pulled my hair straight back in a pompadour with a knot at the back.

I had one pair of what I called "low" shoes, but on ordinary occasions I still wore high-button shoes with gabardine or kid uppers. Under my cousin's influence I'd done away with a number of ruffled petticoats in Washington, as well as corset covers. For that matter I had also abandoned my corset waist and as a result was rather lumpy in the wrong places. I never did care very much about clothes, and when I found a style that I could wear without too much effort or self-consciousness I was inclined to keep right on with it. This, in spite of the fact that years after I left the university a dressmaker in Columbia, Missouri, having seen my name in the paper a few times, came out with the statement that I had been the first student in town for whom she'd made a hobble skirt. I never contradicted her but her claim seemed unlikely, since even if I'd wanted one I couldn't have afforded a hobble skirt in those days. I was lucky to be covered at all.

I reported for work that first Monday morning in a blue featherweight wool that buttoned down the front to the waist and had a modest V-neck. But from the waist down I must have looked a little like a barrel, for the skirt was decorated with narrow loose bands of material, each one sewn at the belt and the hem. It was my favorite dress— I'd bought it in Cleveland—and I wore it until it was almost in threads.

The publicity office of the interfaith organization was

housed in a loft building and I worked at a desk in a great room with several dozen other young women and men both young and middle-aged.

My duties, as explained to me by the head of the department, were to be chiefly writing, editing and making up a house organ for the interfaith cause. I had to travel to New Jersey to the printer's every week to put my little journal to bed, and while some items were contributed, I wrote most of it and had a very proprietary feeling toward it.

What made our publicity job unique was that it was concerned almost entirely with the doings and sayings of missionaries—missionaries from all parts of the world gathered together to promote religious unity.

I thought this a wonderful idea for I believed with all my heart in religion, and I was glad to hear that my own faith, Baptist, was well represented. Though I was a little disillusioned when I found out for the first time that there were so many brands of Baptists!

Soon I'd met, also working in the vineyard of the Lord, three of the people who were to become lifelong friends. One was Estella Karn, who arrived about a week after me, fresh from a tour with a carnival. I can see her now, a tiny creature, well under five feet, heavy red-brown hair in a great bun, brown eyes eager. She wore a black cartwheel velvet hat, a grass-green cloth suit, white canvas high-button shoes and white cotton stockings. I found afterwards that even with dark shoes she invariably wore the white stockings—said they were more sanitary.

The two other new friends were the Haders, Berta and Elmer, a just-married pair of artists who were engaged to do interfaith drawings for posters and pamphlets.

Stella blew into our loft like a cyclone, overflowing with

vitality and ideas. She was just what the place needed, though at first the missionaries were a little taken aback by her informal ways and show business vocabulary. She always referred to them as "mishes" and spent hours asking them about their lives in Timbuktu, Zanzibar or wherever they came from.

It took me weeks of carefully casual questions to find out that Stella, an orphan made miserable by the treatment of an unkind guardian, had run away from her San Francisco home at sixteen to join a circus, adding a few years on to her actual age in order to get the job, and had gone out immediately as advance press agent.

An editor friend of the interfaith publicity head had recommended her as the best promotion person in the business and he hired her sight unseen at a—to me—fabulous salary, $65 a week. The news of this vast pay had preceded her and we were all prepared to loathe her. But she proved so friendly that we forgave her and acknowledged that she knew more about publicity and promotion than all of us put together.

One of Stella's most ambitious projects was a prayer to be heard round the world. When she described it you could fairly see all the people of the earth gathered together in their own lands just when the sun rose over mountain, desert, forest or plain, intoning in their many languages the same prayer. The missionaries after due consideration thought well enough of the idea to appoint one of their number to produce the prayer. Stella instantly dubbed him her prayer expert.

The poor man—he was rather small and gentle-looking —started out confidently enough, but before many days he was timorously creeping into our loft toward evening with a much corrected, much interlined piece of paper on which was his latest attempt at a "prayer with punch."

Stella admitted that *she* couldn't write a suitable prayer
—but she felt she'd know it when she saw it. Sure enough,
one morning she announced that the prayer expert had
achieved the perfect mixture of piety and punch, accepted
the prayer, a day was appointed and the prayer actually
was said round the world by millions, just as she had
planned.

Meanwhile Max, who continued to ply me with meals,
roses and compliments, suggested that I move out of my
expensive hotel into an old brownstone house on lower
Fifth Avenue that had been made over into one-room
apartments by Mme. Duclos, a Frenchwoman he knew.

I went to look and liked the big living-bedroom with
its two couches that would serve as beds at night, its two-
burner hot plate upon which I could prepare limited
meals, and the adequate bathroom. True, the room cost
$25 a month, a quarter of what I earned, and it looked
out on back yards that were often strung with clotheslines
—but I figured I'd maybe get a raise and certainly I
wouldn't be home much in the daytime.

I was glad of the two couches because Hortense Saunders had decided to resign as woman's editor of the Cleveland *Press* and join me in my attempt to conquer New
York. She would share expenses, at least as soon as she
found a job, and that would help. I was glad, for in spite
of having a good many meals bought for me and cooking
the rest on my hot plate, I found living in New York cost
a lot.

Hortense got to New York a while before Christmas,
and Max immediately introduced her to a Hungarian
friend of his named Michael. Michael was a chemist, making big money at the time. He was generous and forever

sending gifts of candy and fruit and taking us out on parties. He and Max, wanting to show us a really exciting time on our first Christmas in New York, invited us to Delmonico's for Christmas Eve dinner. Delmonico's! I simply couldn't believe it.

I'd heard, of course, of this haunt of Diamond Jim Brady and Lillian Russell. Everybody knew of his gargantuan appetite (three dozen oysters at a sitting and magnums of champagne out of chorus girls' slippers). I'd seen Delmonico's impressive outside but it never occurred to me that anybody would invite me to eat there, or indeed, that I'd ever see the inside.

If it isn't clear by this time that I was about as green and unversed in sophisticated life and its ways as anybody who ever hit New York, then I'd certainly better confess the truth here and now. I tried to act about everything new and startling as if I were used to it, but I couldn't be calm about Delmonico's. What should we wear? That was our immediate problem. I took my tiny hoard and splurged on an evening coat of American Beauty velvet. Then I was ashamed to admit that I'd spent so much money and pretended it was only an old thing my cousin had thrown away.

Stella Karn had also invited Hortense and me to a Christmas Eve party and added hospitably that we might bring anybody we liked. So for two strangers to the city we felt we were doing pretty well.

Hortense and I spent all the night before Christmas Eve washing our hair and buffing our nails. Max and Mike put on white tie and tails for Delmonico's and I even borrowed a bit of rouge from a little jar Hortense kept hidden and discreetly applied it to cheeks and lips. True, I took a washrag and rubbed it all off again for, as I explained to Hortense, the one thing we didn't want, going to a place like Delmonico's, was to look like fast women. I even toned her down a little after we were both dressed —that is, pinned the neck of her blue taffeta so it wasn't quite so low and subdued what my critical inspection convinced me was her too-high color. I wore my leftover college formal, a yellow chiffon with little yellow-centered rose-colored flowers sprinkled over it. Hortense said I looked nice and I assured her that she did, but we were both fidgety because we fully expected to find Delmonico's filled with Society with a capital S. What we had forgotten or at least never considered was that Christmas Eve is a family time. People with homes stay in them, trimming trees, wrapping bundles, having intimate fun together.

So, when we got there, Delmonico's was as empty as a museum at midnight and looked almost as vast. The crystal chandeliers were brightly lighted and we received a welcome from headwaiters beyond our wildest dreams. No wonder—we were literally the only diners in the huge room. Later two groups, obviously part, as we were, of the great unattached, drifted in. It was a wonderful meal but to Max's consternation I didn't like oysters, I didn't like duck running blood and I far preferred a hot fudge sundae to the fresh fruit macédoine, thoroughly ruined for me with a generous outpouring of Kirsch.

So the first part of the evening was something less than a success. And an even greater shock for me was Stella's party on Washington Street at an Armenian café where, as we entered, Stella's circus friend Juno was discovered in the midst of what could only be called a cooch dance. The guests had already finished the unusual Christmas Eve dinner of vine leaves stuffed with pistachio nuts and

33

rice, lamb roasted on skewers, yogurt and honey and nut pastries.

Stella had met Juno in the carnival, and when the two of them got to talking at least two-thirds of what they said was utterly unintelligible to the bystander who had not had carny experience. Stella explained to me that cooch dancing was just Juno's way of making a living, otherwise she was a respectable married woman with a son upon whom she doted and for whose education she was storing away the money earned by her rather grotesque contortions.

With her usual hospitality, Stella in handing out party invitations had included two missionaries as well as office workers and old friends. So it was a strangely mixed gathering and I think perhaps Juno tempered her hip slinging a trifle in deference to the cloth. Some of the guests, however, were soon begging for lessons in cooch dancing and before long the floor was filled with jouncing, bouncing learners, Hortense included. Max and I sat on the sidelines and I'm afraid my expression was prim, maybe even grim.

The second part of Stella's party was more to my taste: we went round the corner to a Greek Orthodox Church for midnight mass. At least this was church, even though of a kind I'd never known and not a word of the service and strange chants could I understand. They went on for hours. Some renegades slipped out, but Hortense and I stayed to the end, getting back to Mme. Duclos' third-floor-back with the milkman. It had certainly been a different Christmas—in the course of a few hours it seemed to me that I'd had about everything New York could offer me. And Christmas Day was such an anticlimax after the excitement that I scarcely felt homesick.

3. Show Biz

IN THE weeks that followed Stella's Christmas party I added all sorts of new and strange words to my vocabulary. Cooch dancer seemed a tough epithet to apply to Juno and I was sort of relieved to find that she could also be called a hip-flinger or a torso-tosser. To my Middle Western mind these seemed milder.

I became acquainted with grifters (actually met at least one in the flesh) —that is, chizzes, or perhaps more intelligibly to the general public, persons in a carnival or circus who take advantage of suckers. My favorite among the phrases I learned from Stella Karn was "winging with the bluebird." That was what she called starting out the circus season after the winter lay-off.

You "joined out" with the circus. You "flivved" or "brodied" when you didn't do well, "knocked 'em bow-legged" when you did. The initiated always spoke of the carnival as a carny and of carnival people as carnies.

Circus performers, whenever they came to town, telephoned Stella and then there were joyous reunions. I had a good chance to study Stella and her friends and their amazing way with English, for more and more she and I were thrown together by our work.

In the middle of winter the organization had a big convention in Atlantic City which we were both sent to cover, and the management provided us with two rooms and connecting bath. Up to this time I had regarded Stella with awe for she was completely at home in a world I never dreamed existed—and besides, she earned $65 a week.

At Atlantic City, however, I began to see her as a rather lonely person under all that brisk energy and after she rescued me from being boiled alive, my whole feeling toward her became much cozier.

I'd never had a hot sea bath before and had looked forward to it with anticipation. In my inexperience I got into the tub, turned on the hot salt water which poured out in a great steaming torrent before I could reach the cold water to dilute it. Luckily Stella came into her room and heard me yelling.

As usual, she was equal to the situation and, wise in the ways of hotel bathtubs, reached through the steam to the cold water faucet. With the other hand she hauled me out, lobster red from head to foot and still screaming.

After that, in the intervals between meetings, we explored together the auction rooms, the fortunetellers' booths, the salt water taffy emporiums, the seafood restaurants, and were even pushed along the boardwalk in a double roller chair. Inevitably, Stella knew not only the man who rolled us but the woman who cut silhouettes and two of the fortunetellers. She had been with each one in some carnival or circus, and I stood around on one foot and then the other while she reminisced with them.

She had a way of saying, when I finally dragged her away from these long sessions, "Biff [or Joe or Liz] is such a *nice* kid." She always asked them to have dinner next time they came to New York and at least once I was upset by overhearing what wasn't my business—a request for quite a big loan which was instantly forthcoming.

The next adventure we shared was one for which she could only brief me, since in the course of it she went south and I went west. The interfaith group decided to send teams of missionaries on the road to explain the aims of the organization. Each team had a member of the publicity department assigned to go along. Stella was in her element and handled her trip exactly as she would have handled a circus.

She warned me: "Don't leave the mishes alone with an editor or reporter for a single minute. Decide what you want them to say and tell them before you let them see anybody. They don't know what news is and they're likely to put reporters off with some of that pious stuff."

We each had four mishes to deal with, and Stella was proud of hers.

"My mishes have a lot of pep and zing," she boasted,

and later she decided that her judgment had been almost too accurate. One of her missionaries, carried away by a spirit of freedom (or something), slipped a note under her door the night they spent in Denver suggesting that she come to his room later that evening. She saved the note and showed it to me. I, who had experienced no such flattering overtures, asked breathlessly, "What did you do?"

"Why, I just ignored it, of course," she answered matter-of-factly. "I bet to this day he wonders if I ever saw it. Or whether the chambermaid swept it up. I treated him just the same next day."

To my amazement, our missionary excursions reminded Stella of the circus. Mostly, I suppose, because we were traveling the same routes she had so often followed when she was publicizing tightrope walkers and tigers instead of religion. We were playing one-night stands, too, but the members of our teams were scheduled to speak in churches instead of performing in tents. My job was to see that everybody was comfortably lodged and fed, that the enterprise got publicity, that we made contact with those in charge of church affairs in each town.

I was able to report to Stella that I kept my mishes in order and stuck with them every minute. I had a handful of papers to prove that we did pretty well publicity-wise, too. She surveyed my harvest of stories and after that I thought she seemed to think better of me.

Also my interest in her friends and her past was so eager and unrestrained that it probably flattered her a little. I never could get enough of this so-different atmosphere. I even made several trips with her to the *Billboard* magazine on Broadway to pick up her mail. For months she never gave her correspondents any other address, for she explained that all circus people and carnies used the *Billboard*—their house organ as *Variety* was the house organ of theatre people and vaudevillians—for a post office.

When the carnies and circus people were on the road, *Billboard*, knowing their itinerary, forwarded mail to them. When they were in New York, they went to the office to pick it up because they usually met old friends and could have a good gossip. I met snake charmers, sword swallowers, fire-eaters, operators of shooting galleries and weighing concessions as well as mellow-voiced spielers. Stella always introduced me as a towny, which of course I was, but she would immediately add that I was all right —a good Joe. And so after a cursory inspection of me, the talk would go on exactly as if I were not there.

I overheard admiring references to some of Stella's exploits which I later would urge her to tell me in full— only translated into words I could understand.

One of her most famous stunts seemed to be connected with "paper." The term made absolutely no sense to me until she explained and I must admit I was rather shocked.

She prefaced her sprightly tale by telling me that circuses are in competition not only with other circuses and carnivals but with any kind of event that people spend money to get in to see. Thus Chatauquas are competitors and so are lectures, and even revival meetings.

"In the spring," Stella pointed out, "you can't get a farmer, busy with plowing and planting, to come into town twice, especially if there's admission involved. So whoever gets there first, gets most of the dough."

The story I thought rather scandalous concerned the time Stella was advance agent for a small circus traveling among little towns in the West. Her job was to arrive about two weeks ahead of the outfit and make arrangements for a place to pitch the tent. Then she would hire local men to slap six-sheets on barns, silos and other buildings throughout the countryside. After that she would try to persuade local merchants to put posters in their windows that would sell tickets on the spot. Her final job was to plant stories in the papers.

This particular spring one of the most famous teams of revivalists was traveling the same circuit—and had hired an advance agent to do approximately Stella's job.

Stella had found, however, that her rival was cutting some ethical corners in an effort to save the crowd for his *divertissement*: he was, in fact, spreading reports that the circus which would precede him had been leaving an epidemic behind, and in some of the communities there was the beginning of a frightened effort to pass a quick ordinance banning circuses entirely.

Landing in one small town where this seed had been planted, Stella succeeded in convincing the proper persons that the report was untrue, but she was angry just the same. She arrived at the local railroad depot still simmering, and her eye lighted on some large bundles which she immediately identified as the revivalists' "paper"— that is, posters, six-sheets and all the rest of his advertising material.

Stella had a railroad credit card which she used when she shipped her own paper to various towns. She produced it now, summoned the baggage master and told him that, because of a change in plan, she wanted these bundles—pointing to the revivalists' paper—shipped on the next train to Moose Jaw, Saskatchewan, the last station on that particular railroad line's connections.

The paper was shipped promptly.

"The revival had to skip that town," Stella concluded with satisfaction. "But we did very well there."

That story flew with the speed of light around Stella's little world of circuses and carnivals. They all applauded, of course. I didn't, but in time I came to accept as best I could Stella's belief that you have to do right according to your own convictions. She respected that obligation in others and expected them to do the same for her. In our long friendship and in all our working together, though she argued me down on many questions, she never tried to change me once she realized it was a matter of principle with me. She was an effective leaven for the way I had been brought up, with the idea that there was no middle ground between good and evil, right and wrong.

My favorite of Stella's circus friends was a small, blond, blue-eyed woman named Mabel Stark, who wrestled at every performance with a tiger. Mabel was a veteran in the first circus Stella worked for. The owner of it, Mabel told me, tossed Stella a mileage book and directed, "Make Bakersfield tomorrow."

That very afternoon even before Bakersfield the recruit had her first circus thrill, for she rode parade dressed in red satin breeches and spangled tunic, perched high on a tiger's cage, with the beasts snarling and chewing at one another inside. Then she lunched in the cookhouse and went for a walk around the hippodrome track with the trained seals. That very day Mabel had been scratched on the shoulder by one of her tigers. Many of the bones in her wrists were mended with strips of silver where they had been snapped by the beasts' fangs at various times.

I first met Mabel as she came out of the cage after one of the bouts with her tiger. She looked calm and unruffled and we went to eat apple pie à la mode at a nearby

41

restaurant. Even the valiant Stella still flinched at the memory of a night when she had ridden 60 miles in an ambulance with Mabel after one of the tigers had practically torn the performer's arm from its socket.

"I had to sterilize the wound by pouring burning acid in it," Stella related, shuddering. "And do you know, that woman never whimpered!"

Mabel always wore white in the arena and looked tinier than ever against the great animals. She often carried baby tigers with her on her trips, feeding them from nursing bottles and putting them to sleep in a hammock by the side of her bed. She said she wasn't afraid of her pets and I believed her. But when we tried to take her uptown once in the subway, she turned pale and almost fainted from claustrophobia.

The morning after she was hired, Stella got up at four o'clock to make Bakersfield, as instructed. Twenty-four hours later the circus was on the front page of both Bakersfield papers with a story about how the local home guard —it was wartime—was intending to study her circus in order to learn to mobilize troops quickly. That was one of the tricks she taught me: tie up publicity with a local angle and you'll get twice the space.

She made 300 towns two weeks ahead of the circus that year, carrying two heavy grips mostly filled with cuts and other press material. She wore crepe underwear, shirtwaists that she didn't have to iron and jersey suits that didn't wrinkle.

"Sometimes I got so hungry for something lacy that I would go to a local department store and buy it," she admitted to me rather wistfully. "But usually I had to give it away for I had no place for frills."

All the newspapers were shorthanded so the ingenious

girl press agent rustled ads for some papers, folded copies
for mailing and wrote filler for others. In return she always got good space and often was used as copy herself—
the girl circus press agent. She enjoyed the stories, but
she really didn't approve of them.

"You are not paid to get yourself in print," she ad-
monished one time when I was briefly being a press agent
and not, in spite of her teaching, a very good one.

I asked if she wasn't lonely, ahead of the show most of
the time and meeting mostly strangers. She just looked
at me.

"Of course I got lonesome," she answered. "Don't you
think I'm human? Sometimes I thought it would be the
most wonderful thing in the world if only I could hear a
friendly voice calling me by my first name."

Then she pulled herself up short and looked ashamed.

"Oh, what am I talking about? I really didn't mind. I
was always busy and I had Cora and Ben with me. Sometimes for fun I would register them at the hotels. Cora
was my portable typewriter and Ben was my alarm clock.
Thanks to Ben I only missed one train in my whole circus
experience. That was in Navasota, Texas, and I was eating
a steak in the station lunchroom and didn't hear the all
aboard."

She rode in cabooses and made friends with everybody
from brakemen to senators. She had cards printed to answer the stories traveling men tell young women they
meet upon their travels. She still had several dozen of
these when I first knew her. She'd had them run off for
her own amusement by a tramp printer she encountered
in Michigan.

One said: *Yes, I know. Your wife doesn't understand
you.*

And another: *I'm sorry that your wife is an invalid.*

She would hand these cards out the minute a man began to tell her a familiar story.

"What would they say?" I asked curiously.

"Oh, if they were good Joes, they looked embarrassed for a minute, then laughed and we got to be friends. Some of the other kind just slunk away."

After she began to drive from town to town in a Hupmobile touring car, she would often borrow somebody from the sideshow to make a few of the towns. One of her favorites was midget Duke John, who was two feet three inches tall (of course Stella herself was under five feet, although she always claimed another inch or so).

In some newspaper offices Duke John made a great hit when he strode in with her, holding onto her finger and announcing grandly: "Mr. Editor, meet the wife!"

The Duke, according to Stella, had a fiendish temper and when he lost it, would bite the legs of anybody who had angered him—the legs being the only part of his enemies he could reach.

When she was driving alone, Stella took the precaution of arming herself with a water pistol which she filled with water and red pepper. She claimed it was for skunks, but I think she had some trepidation too about the humans she might chance to meet on lonely roads.

Actually, she was a fearless person about most things but she had one great terror: cats. Even the smallest kitten looked to her like a monster. She would shriek, "See those great big eyes!" and shrink away as far as she could. It even upset her to see a picture of a panther or a leopard in a magazine, but for some curious reason she never seemed to mind lions and tigers.

She had a real affection for snakes, even boa constrictors.

44

And when she happened to be in a town with the rest of the circus the boa constrictor's guardian would bring the snake's voluminous hot water bottle to be filled with hot water from Stella's hotel tap.

Her fear of some of the big cats was one reason she never forgot the night when an animal trainer named Martha turned her back for a second on a pair of leopards she had raised from cubs.

They leaped for her throat and tore it, but Martha managed to put her hands before her face so that she saved her eyes. Helpers got her out of the arena, and she was in the hospital for weeks.

"As soon as she was well," declared Stella admiringly, "she went right back."

In the spring, especially, Stella was nostalgic for the circus. The whole idea of winging with the bluebirds, getting away from the ordinary bothers and perplexities of life, seemed very alluring. But I had the feeling that after such a rootless, roaming existence, she was glad enough to settle down to a regular job and, more important, to a home of her own instead of a hotel room. I often thought that she'd rather talk about being a circus press agent than to have to do it all over again.

4. Chaos and Bananas

TWO women in a one-room apartment, even if they are both near-saints, are bound to have occasional moments of nervous strain. Since I was far from being a saint and Hortense, while better tempered than I, was also human, we had our difficulties now and then. As when both of us wanted to get into the bathroom at the same time, for instance, or one insisted on cooking cauliflower when the other loathed it.

47

Probably, however, the high point in Hortense's and my disagreements came when she arrived home one afternoon, looking flushed and happy. She began at once to plump up cushions and dust off books.

"What's the idea of all the sudden neatness?" I demanded suspiciously.

She turned the other way so that I wouldn't see her pinkening cheeks.

"I'm going out with a new man tonight," she answered much too casually.

"A new man? Where'd you meet him?" I wanted to know at once.

In all our goings and comings, I was the one who made the rules and insisted on the proprieties. I know now that I was a sadly inhibited young woman, but I had no doubt then that I was completely in the right and that my rules of behavior ought to be followed by every respectable girl.

Hortense didn't answer at once, and when I repeated the question she went into the bathroom and pulled tight the curtains that separated it from our bed-living room. By this time I was really upset and followed her with shrill questioning.

At last she reluctantly told me.

"Well, I was waiting for a bus at Fifth Avenue and 28th Street," she admitted, "and this man was standing there.

"He had on glasses," she added parenthetically, as if that would square everything.

"The bus didn't come and it didn't come, and when I opened my purse to get out the fare so as to have it ready, my handkerchief fell out. He picked it up, I thanked him and . . . well, we got to talking."

"Hortense Saunders," I screamed, "you spoke to a strange man on the street?"

She went on hastily: "Well, he was born in Nebraska and he has a job with Warner Brothers, in the publicity department."

I was registering more and more disapproval in spite of the reassuring glasses and birthplace, for a job with a motion picture company sounded pretty loose to me. Hortense accused, "You weren't introduced to Max, either, except by my letter. And what do you think? Jack's writing a piece for the *Saturday Evening Post*. He was a prisoner of the Germans in the war, and he and two other fellows had a miraculous escape. The *Post* hasn't exactly told him they'll take his article but they're going to look at it. And when he found out that I'd worked on a newspaper, he said he'd like me to see if the punctuation and everything is all right."

My severe expression relaxed a little. After all, if the *Saturday Evening Post* was interested . . .

"What's his name?" I demanded.

"Jack Hastings," she said almost proudly. "Don't you think that's a nice writing name?"

"He ought to have a middle initial," I observed judicially, determined not to approve altogether. "About Max, that was different. You knew all about him. . . ."

How wrong I was, we found out some months later, when Max had to confess to a great deception. But I unquestionably felt at the time that I was much more virtuous than my friend. Why Hortense put up with me, I can't imagine. She was a city girl—she'd grown up in Cleveland—and, compared to me, she'd led a pretty sophisticated life. Why she let a little country girl boss her, I don't know. I suppose it was partly because I was not only overwhelmingly rigid in my ideas about the moral code of conduct but also, in spite of my timidity and indecisiveness about

49

most things, when it came to what I believed to be right I was absolutely determined.

"I'll tell you what," I now relented, "I'll stay right here until this Jack comes tonight and I'll find out about him and make him realize that you're not a young girl alone in the city."

That's exactly what I did, too. When Jack arrived, metal-rimmed glasses, high stiff collar and black derby clutched in hand, I fixed him with a stern eye and at once began an inquiry into his antecedents, his financial status, even his ambitions. It would have served me right if he'd told me to mind my own business but he didn't. In fact, he answered very politely and then, with a frankness I've never been able to subdue, I told him that I thought he and Hortense had behaved very unconventionally and that I just wanted to be sure he was all right before Hortense went out with him. I added portentously, "A girl can't be too careful in a strange city."

He laughed then and even said he thought I was right. He assured me that he could furnish references if necessary from his home town minister. I had to laugh, too, at that, and they went off happily to the Palais Royal where they stopped for more hours than I approved.

Hortense and I were both tired of the one-room apartment after two months of it and Stella Karn, who up to then had been living in a cheap theatrical hotel, also longed for a change. The three of us decided to move to Greenwich Village, abode of painters, writers, poets— or so we hoped.

Apartments-to-rent section of *The New York Times* in hand, we tramped Village streets, climbing hundreds of flights of steep stairs that led into lofts and garrets in which geniuses are supposed to work and starve.

Finally we settled on a third-floor walkup on Fourth Street, owned by an elegant gentleman both of whose names were reminiscent of Old New York, Stuyvesant Wainwright.

We had a living room, two bedrooms, dining room, kitchen and bath. Most of the furniture was a little wobbly because, as Mr. Wainwright pointed out, it was family antiques. Before our tenure ended, the record of broken chairs and slightly injured guests had reached record proportions. One fat gentleman caller of mine waiting for me to finish dressing sat too hard on a Chippendale side chair. We heard a crash and rushed in to find my date flat on his back with one leg straight up in the air. We had to summon an ambulance because the other leg was broken.

"Sty," as we affectionately called our landlord behind his back, was astonishingly philosophical about such disasters. The only trouble was, he never gave us anything to take the place of the smashed equipment, so pretty soon if more than two were gathered together, somebody had to sit on the floor. However, this was standard Village practice and nobody seemed to mind.

We drew straws for rooms. By a turn of fortune, I got the rather respectable-sized bedroom. Hortense had the smaller hall room—really a little box just big enough for a single bed, small dresser and one chair. Poor Stella uncomplainingly took what was left—a couch in the living room. But then, as we pointed out, she was the smallest of the three and likely to get in at two or more in the morning, so the couch was really more convenient for her.

Of us all, she enjoyed the place most. She was a few years older than we were and for some time she had been living in hotels all over the country and eating indifferent restaurant meals. She was thrilled with the chance to cook and to our surprise proved to have a real gift for it.

The difficulty was that she couldn't pass a delicatessen without stopping to add to our supplies. This was all very well for her, with her $65 a week. But Hortense—who had a small publicity job by now—and I were not so flush and we found most extravagant all the lovely things in glass—enormous peaches, pickled walnuts, artichoke hearts (I barely knew what an artichoke looked like much less what you did with their hearts.)

At least one of the beautiful glass jars of peaches contained brandy in addition to the fruit and for a long time Stella and Hortense would embarrass me by telling about the day they came home and found me busy at the kitchen sink, scrubbing canned peaches.

"What on earth are you doing?" shrieked Hortense, reaching out a restraining hand, for this was one of her favorite desserts.

Without even looking up, I went right on scrubbing, crying angrily, "I'm washing the brandy off these peaches. It says right on the jar they have brandy on them and they've been soaking in it for goodness knows how long. I don't know how I'll ever get it off."

Usually, Hortense and Stella ganged up on me. They couldn't resist teasing me about my naïve ways. But there was one time when Stella and I executed a plot that really infuriated our gentle Hortense. Her birthday was coming up and Mike, always one to remember anniversaries generously, asked Stella and me what she would like most to have.

For quite a while we had been worried about our icebox—or rather, Sty's—which leaked in about three places. Without even looking at each other we earnestly and simultaneously assured Mike that what Hortense wanted more than anything in the whole wide world was a new icebox. And that is exactly what she got, white and shining, a truly handsome gift, just out of the factory and delivered at 10 A.M. on her birthday.

She realized instantly that we must be responsible and she first gave us a tongue-lashing and then didn't speak to us for three days. Some time later she came to me one morning with a pair of shoes in her hand. She was almost in tears.

"Just look at this," she commanded, pointing to a hole worn all the way through one sole. "I actually can't afford even half-soling, much less a new pair of shoes if Stella keeps on buying all those things she sees in windows!"

While I felt much as she did, I also thought I understood Stella's urge to homemake, and so I promised to see if I could explain our situation without hurting our housemate's feelings. Stella listened composedly to my rather halting dramatization of our predicament. Then she nodded her head briskly. "That's all right," she said, "I'll pay for them myself."

This was typical and I might have expected it. I set to work then to convince her that ours had to be a three-way split, that Hortense and I must keep up our end if we were to be self-respecting, and that the only cure for the difficulty was for her to resist temptation. She finally agreed that she would do her best to pass by on the other side of the street but I suspect that she never told us when she found temptation too much for her and simply paid out of her own pocket.

She did, suddenly, seem to make an effort towards economy by having one-dish meals: macaroni and cheese; baked beans in individual earthen bowls with pork chops on top; and a masterpiece we called Chaos, also in the individual Mexican bowls. This was made of canned tamales (Hortense and I had never heard of them, but Stella knew them from New Mexico), canned corn, green peppers and pimientos moistened with chili sauce and a slice or two of bacon crisped on top.

We all got a good many invitations to dinner partly because we frequently invited our various young men to share our meals and it was the custom then for the male not only to reciprocate such attentions but go the girl one or two better.

Max never shared the Chaos and macaroni meals. I knew they weren't exactly his style but still I thought we ought to invite him. I was puzzled that both Hortense and Stella always found some excuse not to have him and I noticed that they weren't very friendly when he came to fetch me for an engagement.

Their coldness became so apparent that I finally asked them outright what was wrong. They evaded and denied, but they looked so guilty while they did it that I knew something was really on their minds. So I demanded they tell me.

My two friends stammered and hesitated and sat one on each side of me as if to support me in my hour of trial. If they had been breaking the news of a death they couldn't have been more anxious. They knew that I took everything hard and they feared I'd take this hardest of all.

"Max is married," Stella finally blurted. "His wife lives right up in the Bronx."

"That's not true!" I flatly contradicted.

My friends said they hadn't believed it either, at first. A woman at Stella's Christmas party had told Stella because she thought since he seemed so attentive to me I ought to know that he had a wife. After that, Stella and Hortense had made other inquiries. It was true, they reiterated—sorrowfully and angrily.

I said it couldn't be so. I cried. I reviled them for false friends. I said Max wouldn't behave like that. I reminded them that he had often begged me to marry him.

"Well, just ask him," suggested the practical Stella.

With my usual cowardice about unpleasantness, I didn't want to. For several days I refused to talk to him on the telephone and I broke the appointments we already had, but finally over Sunday breakfast at the Brevoort I confronted him with the charge.

He was raising a forkful of the famous Brevoort chicken hash to his lips when I rather apologetically announced that I had something to check with him. He put down the hash untasted and a look I couldn't read came over his face. I think I knew then, but I went ahead anyway telling him what I'd heard.

His liquid brown eyes filled with tears and I believe he was genuinely torn with remorse as he confessed that my friends had told the truth.

I've often wondered since what he would have done if I'd taken him up on some of the countless occasions when he urged, "Let's go right down to City Hall now and get a marriage license." I finished my chicken hash. Then we parted forever.

Stella's choice in men leaned to the Orient. She was taking international law at Columbia University and a Chinese professor and a Siamese fellow student were around the house a good deal at this time. One night when we'd expected only them, a cousin of Stella's turned up and was promptly urged by the hospitable Miss Karn to stay to dinner.

This meant that we were short one bowl of Chaos, which with a salad was the entire meal. Stella and Hortense conferred privately and then called me into my bedroom. "You'll have to go to bed," they asserted with finality. "There isn't enough Chaos to go around, so we'll just say you aren't feeling well."

They all but undressed me and stuck me into my bed —with me at first dazed, then mad. After they had left me and shut the door, I could hear the clatter of cutlery and cheerful voices out in the dining-room-kitchen. I could smell the savory Chaos, too. I lay there getting more and more furious until suddenly I decided to take steps. I knew our little grocery store across the street kept open until 8:30 and I flung on a raincoat over my nightgown, screwed up my hair and rushed down the two flights of stairs to the street. In the store, my good friend Steve looked anxiously at my face.

"Whassa mattah?" he probed, but for once I did not stop to talk.

"I just came in to buy some bananas," I assured him haughtily in order to forestall further questions. "I think I'll have that whole bunch right there. And charge it, please, to Stella."

With that I slung an entire stalk of bananas over my shoulder and staggered out. (I forgot to say that I was wearing overshoes that flopped because they hadn't been fastened.) I was away and half across the street before Steve could even catch his breath, much less offer to deliver the bananas. I didn't want help. I wanted to suffer so everybody would be sorry for me. I banged up the stairs, the banana stalk scraping and making a frightful racket, slammed doors with all my might and retreated to my bedroom to eat bananas. For once even the imperturbable Stella was humiliated by my behavior.

"You have to remember that Orientals have a different standard of manners from ours," she reminded me sternly after the visitors had left. "They will feel that you were being inhospitable."

By that time I was practically comatose from too many bananas and could only mutter sullenly, "I was hungry and I don't see anyway why I had to be the one to go to bed!"

"Because you don't like company," my housemates reminded me callously.

It was true that sometimes I did exile myself to my bedroom when the invitees were not chosen, or at least approved of, by me.

Almost the only people I really liked to talk to were writers. Hortense more or less went along with me on this, but Stella's tastes ranged from her missionaries through tattooed ladies, scientists, inventors, a reformed burglar (though even I was interested in him) to a millionairess from San Francisco who had once backed financially a march on City Hall organized by Stella and participated in by inhabitants of the red-light district. This was part, Stella explained, of a slum clearance crusade. And very effective, too. The reminiscing of Stella and her co-crusader especially horrified me.

A too-candid friend reading these pages as I write them has been shocked, she says, by some of the contradictions in myself that I have revealed.

"I begin to suspect your character," she mused, looking at me accusingly.

I don't know precisely what *she* means, but I am quite

well aware, not only of the contradictions but of the ugly blemishes in my character. There is no question that my plan for myself was perfection and I flogged myself when I fell short, as fall short I continually did.

During all my early days in New York I was constantly popeyed with astonishment and disapproval, but I cannily concealed my feelings until I felt it was safe to voice them. Then I spoke out with irritating righteousness. And invariably before I knew it I was guilty of worse deeds than those I most piously deplored.

Snobs and climbers I particularly dislike, yet in my time I've been both. I was once even ashamed of my adored mother. That's about as low as anybody can get. I remember, just before she came on for her first visit to New York, lying awake worrying about what my friends would think of her.

I knew what she was—a wonderful, intelligent woman of sweetness and character who didn't know much about city ways, didn't care about clothes, and although in only her late forties, had work-worn hands and bowed shoulders from the hard life of a farm.

I suppose it was my own feeling of inferiority and my immaturity—I was much less adult than I should have been for my years—that made me fear that people whose opinion I valued highly might not recognize my mother for what she was.

I was also afraid the city and its people might overwhelm her. As it turned out, I had all my worries for nothing. From the start, my mother showed herself adequate for anything. I met the wrong train and she successfully wrestled with the situation by appealing to a porter who took her to the Traveler's Aid. A kind woman there checked my address, got Mother into a taxicab and when I frantically telephoned to Stella and Hortense, my mother was at that very moment sitting in our most comfortable chair drinking a cup of coffee. (Incidentally, my housemates were smoking cigarettes when she rang the bell. They rushed with them to the bathroom and after that, for the rest of her visit, they always retired to the bathroom to smoke.)

As for my friends, the more sophisticated and city-bred they were—both men and women—the more they seemed to like my mother. They positively fought over her. Every day somebody borrowed her for something—a flower show, a symphony concert or a Broadway play. My mother loved them all and confided to me that she thought they were a little homesick.

One of her hostesses took her to Coney Island for a day and they got into a show that had dancers with almost no clothes on.

"Poor girls," Mama said sadly. "How glad I am that Sister doesn't have to do that for a living."

In spite of the strict way in which she had been brought up, nothing seemed to shock her, not even seeing people drinking cocktails. I truly believe she could have taken even a speakeasy calmly. Long afterwards a woman I knew well told me that she had confided to my mother a story of wrongdoing that she had never told anybody else.

"I was a little worried about what she'd think of me, but I just had to tell somebody," she explained. "Your mother's expression as she looked at me was so compassionate that I knew she was sorry for me and understood. My burden was less from then on."

On the way home from a luncheon with Hortense, Mama's cab collided with another car and the taxi man accompanied her up our two flights of stairs to explain

59

and to assure himself that his passenger was all right. I was as scared as if the accident were still threatening her and asked anxiously if she was hurt.

She said she was shaken up a little bit but otherwise was feeling fine. After the taxi man had gone, I inquired, "What were you doing, Mama, when the men were arguing and the policeman came?"

"I was just sitting there waiting," she said.

"Weren't you afraid?" I probed.

She raised her head to look at me very deliberately in a way she had: "No, daughter, I wasn't afraid," she answered serenely, as she had often done before when I had asked a question she considered unnecessary.

Although I had been planning that we would have my mother's hot biscuits, fried chicken, cream gravy and apple dumplings every day while she was there, she was invited out so much that she finally had to request a let-up in the festivities in order to cook a meal for us and have a little visit with me.

She evidently had a good time, for after that she came every year—every year that I wasn't too broke to send her the fare, that is.

5. I Become A Sob Sister

ABOUT the time Mama went back to Missouri after that first visit, rumors began to fly about that the interfaith organization was shaky. There were stories of disputes and disagreements among those at the head and even hints that the substantial sums in back of the enterprise might soon be withdrawn.

Stella, the optimist, pooh-poohed such suggestions. But I brooded over them, and so it came as no real surprise to me when we were summoned one by one to the office of the publicity department to be told that our jobs would end in two weeks.

With my usual tendency to look on the tragic side, I assured everybody who would listen that I would never, never find another job. About this time, too, our landlord came to tell us something that we already knew, for we'd read it in the newspapers—his son had eloped with Edith Gould, one of THE Goulds.

Her family, displeased at the elopement, had temporarily disinherited her, so Sty needed our apartment for the young couple to live in. Since we had no lease, he gave us a week's notice. But before we could get out his daughter-in-law moved in with twenty or thirty trunks which so filled the little apartment that we could no longer reach the stove to prepare a final meal.

The new Mrs. Wainwright looked at us with considerable interest and some awe.

"Do you mean that you actually earn your living?" she inquired rather skeptically. We assured her that we did, and she marveled: "And you do all your own work, too. I don't know how to cook or sweep or anything." Since her young husband hadn't much money, it looked as if she would have to learn. We used to wonder how she came out.

Hortense, who still had a job, chose to move to a smaller apartment in the Village and sold the birthday icebox, generously splitting the proceeds three ways. Stella and I, after a long search, found a really inexpensive walk-up.

The first few days in our new home in Chelsea, a section of New York on the extreme West Side, were nightmarish —filled with the smell of cheap paint, the shrill ringing of an unmusical doorbell and much trudging up four steep flights of stairs.

The apartment was unfurnished, so Stella and I, now jobless, bought a few pieces of secondhand furniture from a dingy rundown junk store nearby and carried most of them home ourselves.

We went all the way to the Bronx to get our beds, springs and mattresses because a low-priced store there also gave long-term credit. The clerk promised immediate delivery but days—and nights, too—went by with no beds. We put pillows and quilts on the floor and tried to sleep. Luckily, we were young and healthy so that we had less backache and general misery than might have been expected.

The day the beds were finally delivered we looked forward to a long, peaceful night of undisturbed sleep. Hortense came up from the Village that evening to see how we were getting on. She viewed the new beds, we had something to eat, and then both Stella and I began to yawn in Hortense's face. She obligingly took the hint and departed. But hardly were we settled happily for the night in our new beds than the doorbell rang. It was Hortense.

She was embarrassed. "I've left my key inside my apartment," she said apologetically. "I'm locked out and the superintendent is away for the night so there's nobody to let me in. May I sleep on your floor?"

I'd have let her do it, too, but good old Stella, soul of hospitality, wouldn't hear of such a thing.

"Of course you'll take my bed," she insisted. They compromised by both sleeping in Stella's single bed.

We had three tiny rooms (besides a minuscule kitchen and bathroom) but we never did get together enough furniture for more than two. The third little cubbyhole, which would have been the living room if we'd had anything to put in it, we called the genius room and I kept my typewriter on an upended orange crate meaning at any minute to start my great novel. The genius room became the repository for empty boxes, pieces of string, newspapers that Stella insisted on saving and anything else that we needed to hide.

Even the gallant Stella got a bit low in her mind during this period, and I was absolutely without hope. But as soon as we were settled, if you can call it that, we both started frantically answering advertisements for "girls wanted."

We were really and truly very close to being completely broke, so much so that we divided every bit of food in half and then rationed it rigidly. We found one bread that made more slices and bought that one from then on. The one-dish meals came in handy, too. We were so hungry at times that we held longing conversations about what we would eat when we finally got jobs. Stella was all for beefsteak and French fries, but I, nostalgic as usual, yearned for one of my mother's Missouri dinners—crisply fried chicken, cream gravy, hot biscuits with butter melting into their hearts, and hot apple pie with cream so thick you had to spoon instead of pour.

When you're that broke you don't see people: you don't want to. We didn't even have a telephone so that nobody knew how to reach us, and except for Hortense we were shut off from the world.

I thought of my lost Max with a good deal of regret during this hungry period for he really had taste in food and was a good spender, too.

Actually, I was very lucky to have Stella to share my financial miseries. In the first place, she had been broke before and, both from experience and a naturally optimistic nature, did not consider it to be more than a passing phase. As a veteran, she knew ways of cutting corners and making do.

When we were closest to the bottoms of our purses, Stella's greatest regret was that we were not living in Los Angeles, which she maintained was a wonderful place for scrounging free meals without loss of dignity.

A few years before, she had been temporarily embarrassed when the circus was in winter quarters and needed no advance agent. In fact, she was down to pennies. One day, leaving the downtown post office after a fruitless inquiry at General Delivery, she passed a little real estate office advertising Malibu Beach building sites. The prospective buyers were driven out to the Pacific Ocean-front development in midmorning to look at the land, and as a further come-on were promised box lunches so that the trip would not deprive them of their midday meal.

Stella instantly became interested in beach-front real estate. And she lived for a solid week on the box lunches of a half-dozen real estate developers.

"It was fine," she recalled. "They had to give pretty good lunches because most of their customers were retired farmers from Iowa, and they were accustomed to big noonday meals. We used to have fried chicken, lots of bread, hot coffee, even desserts." Then she added wistfully: "I've looked around, but they don't do that here— not even when they want you to look at property on Long Island. These subways make distances too short."

Stella was luckier than I jobwise. She could type better. So she was able to get a day's work now and then transcribing businessmen's letters from a dictaphone. One night she came panting up the four flights, jubilant. I thought, of course, she had got just the right permanent job. But no, it was something she'd bought.

65

"Look!" she exulted. "Look what I have!"

I looked, and almost fainted. What she had was a small paper pamphlet with the words *Dream Book* written on the paper cover.

"Now we'll know what all our dreams mean," she said excitedly. "I bought it with a quarter tip the man I worked for today gave me."

I hate to think of the exasperated scolding I gave that poor woman. I reminded her of our near-penniless state, described our prospects as nil, and "idiot" and "spend-thrift" were just two of the milder words I used to characterize her.

She didn't lose her temper, though she certainly had one to lose. But her face fell and all the happiness went out of her eyes.

"It only cost a quarter and the man gave the quarter to me for a tip," she kept repeating.

But this was no explanation for me. I reminded her over and over what a quarter would have bought. Repeated again and again how broke we were. I certainly did everything I could to spoil her pleasure in her purchase. But Stella being Stella, later that evening she was thumbing through the pages with undiminished zest. She even tried to read some of them to me, convinced that I would eventually be as charmed as she was by her find.

Stella's course in international law at Columbia was paid up ahead so she continued to go there many evenings. Then when she came home she would put our family wash to soak in the bathtub and sometimes, tired out with job hunting and worrying, we would both go to sleep leaving the clothes soaking and the bathroom light wastefully on. The idea was that we would get up later and finish the washing.

66

This practice apparently was responsible for a note that we got from the renting agent of the house:

> We've had complaints about excessive noise and disturbances all night that seem to originate in the apartment occupied by you. Will you please call at 4 o'clock on Tuesday at this office and discuss this matter.

For once Stella and I reacted in much the same way to a situation. We were furious. Since we moved in there had been nobody but ourselves in our apartment with the exception of Hortense and two policemen, summoned off their beat (policemen traveled in pairs in that location) by Stella when she found a broken window catch which made her suspect burglars.

Stella wanted to go right down then and tell the man off, but I insisted that we wait and keep the appointment. Stella raged we could sue them. She said it was false accusation and would blacken our characters. I pleaded with her not to bring me into court. I told her about the time my father had knocked down Mr. Tom Collier on Main Street in Paris, Missouri, in an argument over a fence (their farms adjoined) and they'd both been hauled into court. I still remembered my mother's tears and her feeling that we were all disgraced forever, though nothing came of it except a good talking-to by the judge. This would be just as humiliating. But Stella kept on threatening.

On Tuesday we put on our best clothes—I think I even carried a pair of gloves somebody had given me although I had never worn gloves in my life, summer or winter.

"At least we look respectable," I commented as we set forth.

Evidently the agent agreed with me. I'll never forget

the look of consternation on his face when we walked into his office, Stella leading, poised for battle, outrage in every line of her body.

Before she could begin the attack, the now embarrassed agent said placatingly, "Ladies, it's evident there's been a mistake. Now that I see you, I know you could never be responsible for the reports we got."

After one stunned moment we were both madder than ever, though for different reasons. Stella, who loved a battle, was suddenly deprived of the chance to wage one, for though she kept on talking about false accusations and suing him, the agent's obvious dismay and apologetic manner slowed her down. You can't fight with somebody who keeps assuring you that you are right and apologizing to boot.

My anger was because he had taken one look at us and decided that we weren't the type for wild, all-night parties. No woman likes to be thought as unexciting as all that. Of course I certainly did want to be considered respectable, but I had been in New York for about six months by this time and thought I had grown quite sophisticated.

As we left, Stella still muttering threats of suit, the agent was promising to look into the wild parties. Later, he reported—per agreement—that an apartment on the same floor as ours was occupied by two women of, he said conservatively, "high spirits." They gave parties almost every night and almost every night the parties reached a peak where glasses were broken and merriment approached riot proportions. The complainants, of course, had seen our innocent bathroom light and had jumped to the wrong conclusion.

This explained some of the untoward sounds that had

disturbed us at night, such as the ringing of our doorbell at one or two in the morning though nobody was there when we answered. The bumping sound that had been a mystery for a long while was finally cleared up when we opened the door towards dawn one morning and found a man lying there, apparently asleep.

Investigation revealed that he lived on the floor above and had collapsed because of a habit of taking too much to drink. We didn't know what to do about him, so just left him to sleep it off. It developed later that he was rather a well-known poet and, in fact, one morning we found a poem slipped under our door. We never knew whether he left it on purpose as part payment for our doorstep or whether it had just dropped out of his pocket as he "rested" there. The poem was a sonnet addressed to Julia.

A night or two later I came in, tired, utterly discouraged, almost ready to give up the struggle. I'd been turned away by so many stone-faced office boys in newspaper offices that I doubted I'd ever get to talk to a real editor. Years later Mrs. Ogden Reid of the New York *Herald Tribune* told me of finding among some old papers a letter from Dean Walter Williams of the Missouri School of Journalism recommending me highly to her husband.

"Why didn't you ever come to see him?" she asked.

I laughed a little and sighed a little, remembering how often I'd tried to get by the office boy at the *Tribune*. In my wildest imaginings it wouldn't have occurred to me to ask to see Mr. Ogden Reid himself. The city editor was the most I dared hope for, and he, according to the office boy, was always just getting out an edition.

That day I looked in the mailbox, hoping for a letter from home, and found instead a thin envelope with a return address in the upper left-hand corner—NEW YORK EVENING MAIL, CITY HALL PLACE. My hands were shaking so that I could hardly hold the letter, much less open it.

The *Mail* was one of two papers I hadn't yet visited because I was concentrating on morning papers. *Why* should the *Evening Mail* be writing to me?

I climbed the four flights, my heart pounding. If only Stella would be at home—but she wasn't! I held the letter gingerly to the light. No clue to its contents. I turned it over and over and scrutinized the typewritten address. I was really afraid to open it. But finally I did.

I looked at the signature first. Hal Reynolds. Where had I heard that name? Well, he must know me because the letter began "Dear Mary Margaret— Since I left the publicity department of the interfaith organization I have been made city editor of the *Evening Mail*."

Then came the incredible part: "We need a girl who can cover fires dramatically and I thought at once of you. The salary will be $40 a week and if you are interested in the job, come to see me here at the *Mail* office."

Instantly I was in a panic. The letter had been forwarded from Fourth Street. It had already been delayed. Suppose he had found somebody else by this time! It was now 6 o'clock. Did city editors of afternoon newspapers work after six? Should I go down and telephone from the corner drugstore? No, he said *Come to see me.* I would be there at seven in the morning. Did a New York city editor get in at seven? No matter, I could wait.

Then came typical McBride second thoughts. Maybe he had mixed me up with somebody else. Could I really cover fires dramatically? What did that mean, anyway? Would Stella never come home? Maybe I'd better call

Hortense, she'd worked on a newspaper much longer than I had.

I couldn't sit still so I walked the floor and by the time Stella arrived breathless from the four flights I was crying gently, whether from joy or apprehension I hardly knew. I couldn't even tell her the news—words wouldn't come. I just thrust the letter at her. She read it quickly and was instantly ready to celebrate. For her, it was all a fact accomplished: as far as she was concerned I already had a job at $40 a week covering fires dramatically.

"I was paid $3 today," she announced. "Let's go and spend it all at Charles' for beefsteak and French fries."

Then, remembering my preferences, she added kindly, "You can have ham."

Cautious as usual, I protested. "I haven't got the job yet. And besides, part of that beef stew was left from yesterday. We'll stay right here and eat it."

We did, too. But it was a celebration anyway. Stella went out and bought a package of our favorite cookies for dessert—Coconut Dainties, they were called. Luck was certainly with us that night, for there were 16 cookies in the box instead of the 15 we were sometimes disappointed to find. One cookie matters when you're broke. We ate the whole 16 recklessly, 8 apiece.

There wasn't much sleep for me that night—not even as much as when we were sleeping on the floor before the beds came. By 5:30 I was taking a bath and had already washed my hair. My nails were cut down practically to the quick. I pressed my favorite of the dresses Gladys had given me, a peach-colored challis with a guimpe which certainly wasn't appropriate for that time in the morning but I thought it looked impressive, and Stella was never any help as an advisor on clothes. She got up though and made me some breakfast which she insisted that I eat. I didn't want to eat, of course. I thought I should never want to eat again if I didn't get that job.

It was a long trip by subway down to the City Hall station. The *Mail* was at 25 City Hall Place. I wanted to ask Stella to go with me, but thought it didn't look very courageous for a would-be reporter to be accompanied. Evidently Stella thought so too, for she didn't offer.

There was one of those stony-faced office boys. But when I asked for Mr. Reynolds and said that he had told me to come, the boy's face relaxed and he led me into the city room and over to the corner where Hal Reynolds was sitting. He knew me right away. He hadn't mixed me up with somebody else at all. And as far as he was concerned, the job was already mine—on trial, at least—at $40 a week. He said I could go to work at once or wait until tomorrow, and I said that I'd go to work right away.

For my first assignment Mr. Reynolds sent me up to the Biltmore Hotel, where society debutantes had taken over for a day and were serving as bellhops and waitresses for charity.

When I came back I crumpled up 12 leads before I found one that would do. I won't quote it for it couldn't have been more banal, but I imagine I was about the happiest girl in the world that night.

I was in New York City and on a newspaper!

6. I Cover That Fire

MY NEW city editor said nothing more to me just then about covering fires dramatically, but I thought a good deal about the subject. After all, the letter had said that was why they wanted me.

Even without fires, I immediately became the paper's sob sister. I loathed the title and fumed inwardly every time I heard one of the men use it, which they did, far too often. Except for Grace Robinson, the woman's page editor, I was at first the only woman on the paper, and so it was expected that every time there was a sad story or one that involved my sex I would be sent out.

The assumption that I was only good for one type of story made me feel like a sort of second-class citizen, but I was still unmodern enough to like the fact that even in this busy, noisy news factory the men behaved with considerable chivalry. They never told dirty stories or swore when I was around—often I'd see one gesture to another to warn him of my approach—and they often took me out for coffee or a sandwich. They would have been shocked, I'm sure, if I had offered to pay my share, and it would never have occurred to me.

Of course they didn't put on their coats, or take off their hats, or get up when I came in, but it was clear that they regarded me as a good woman and a newspaperman of the time was bound to respect and protect a good woman.

It was nearly a year before I broke out of my sob sister ghetto to get a real assignment, and it was one of these stories that caused the greatest outburst of chivalry. I was covering a murder trial in Brooklyn. The judge was named Cropsey and he was known as a fairly tough judge, particularly where courtroom etiquette was concerned. All this I found out afterwards.

I had such a good reputation for sedate deportment that nobody thought to warn me that there are special rules of conduct to be observed in a courtroom.

It was about the second day and court had just resumed after the noon recess. While we were out I had bought an early edition of the *Mail,* and after the judge's entrance I opened the paper to the third page to see if they'd used my picture with my feature story. I really didn't intend to read it, just to look at the setup.

I never even got time to do that. Suddenly I heard Judge Cropsey roar, "Take that woman out and see that she stays out of my court!"

There was a rustle in the courtroom and I looked up with pleasurable interest, hoping for a little excitement. To my horror, the judge's finger was pointing directly at me, and instantly there converged upon me four bailiffs who led me limp and unprotesting from the room.

Without saying a word, they deposited me in the hall and left me. Standing there motionless, clutching my newspaper and my pencil and pad, I began after my unfailing custom in time of stress to cry. And not knowing what else to do, I stumbled out of the building and took the subway back to City Hall. Luckily I was in an almost empty car for I bawled every instant of the way.

As I walked into the city room, the humiliation of what had happened broke over me afresh and I began to sob out loud. Instantly most of the men in the place rushed toward me, asking concerned questions, trying to offer comfort. It was quite a while before I could stammer out the full details of my story. When I finished, the men all looked as though they could cry too, and one used a word about Judge Cropsey that he had never before permitted himself to utter in my presence.

Most upset of all was Oliver Cromwell of Kentucky, who was sitting in that day on the city desk. His walrus mustaches quivered and his voice, too, as he cried angrily, "He can't do that to you. I ought to go right over there and take my horsewhip to him."

He looked so fierce and sounded so determined that for

a terrible moment I was really afraid he was going to do it and began to beg him not to. He finally compromised by telling me to take the rest of the day off and muttering that the *Mail* would certainly see that Judge C. never got any good publicity in our newspaper.

Not a man there explained what I learned years later from Cynthia Lowry, a newspaperwoman friend who had covered many courts in New York State.

"It's one of those unwritten rules that the only newspaper you can read in a courtroom is the *Law Journal*," she explained. "Some judges make a big thing of it. They'll put anybody out who violates it."

City Editor Reynolds left the *Mail* very soon after he'd seen himself justified (I hope) for hiring me to cover fires dramatically. Though maybe I'm bragging on myself, as we say in Missouri, by claiming that I described with drama the dreadful tenement fire in the Bronx that he sent me to report.

News of the disaster came into the office late in the morning. It was a five-alarm fire and my usually calm city editor was excited when he called me over to give me the assignment.

"Do a good story," he exhorted with the same kind of urgency in his voice that a football coach uses in his final pep talk before the team goes out to face its main rival.

I looked to make sure I had my precious police card hidden in the band of my hat (I was still carrying a dollar bill or two there also), grabbed a handful of copy paper and three or four soft pencils before I flew out the door.

The subway seemed to take forever to get up to the Bronx, and as I ran out of the Fordham station I saw a taxicab, threw thrift to the wind and hailed it. Of course, if I had only known I could have put the cost on my expense account. Only I didn't know I had an expense account!

Hurrying toward the blaze, I pulled out my press card—the reporter's sesame. It stated that MARY MARGARET MC-BRIDE *representing the* NEW YORK EVENING MAIL *is entitled to pass police and fire lines wherever formed.* I stuck it in approved journalist's style upright in the hatband so it could be seen easily. And then I proudly crossed my first fire line.

The burning building was old and made of wood. It was crackling like a giant bonfire. Firemen had already pulled out all those who could be rescued and were trying to keep the flames from spreading to other buildings. Ambulances were clanging to and fro and the injured and dead were being carried toward them on stretchers.

I hung around nervously in back of the engines while I mustered my courage. Then I spotted a knot of shabbily dressed men and women standing silent and sad watching the flames and streams of water. Behind the group, and apart, were three old women dressed in shabby black with heavy veils like widows. I walked over and as boldly and sympathetically as I could, began to ask questions.

Two of them just stood staring, like creatures in a trance, but the third answered me in a lackluster voice. They were sisters who had lived in the building all their lives, as had their parents before them. They were dressed in mourning for their mother, who had died a few weeks before. Now they had lost everything.

I talked to others at the fire—firemen who described what the "inferno" was like—gathered statistics of injured and dead, got a statement from the captain as to probable cause. But my real story was the women in black.

I rushed back to the office and began pounding the

typewriter, a copy boy at my elbow to grab each page as it came from the machine. We were getting close to deadline for the *Mail's* final two editions of the day. I made it with seconds to spare and then, grimy and heartsick after the frenzied excitement, started home.

First I thought I might lie down for a while but I was too restless, so I got up again and walked over to Sixth Avenue. I was standing right by a newsstand—not entirely by chance—when a load of final editions of the *Mail* was slapped down. I watched impatiently as the dealer untied the bundle, revealing the top half of the front page. There to my dazzled eyes was revealed my own story in black headlines. Underneath was my name, my full name, in letters that were smaller than the headlines but to my enraptured vision seemed twice as large.

This was great tidings to give to Stella that night, and she had exciting news too. A temporary job that she had been doing for the past few days had turned into a permanent secretaryship if she wanted it. She had been working for Lester Santley, who was in charge of promotion and advertising of the Leo Feist Music Corporation.

A week or so later she came home, looking dazed but triumphant. She had made a mild suggestion to Lester about a story she was copying for him and he had suddenly looked at her hopefully and asked, "Do *you* know how it ought to be?"

She assured him as modestly as she could that she thought she did know and he drew a breath of relief. "Fix it then," he commanded. At the close of the day he told her that she was now in charge of publicity for Leo Feist.

"I'm a musician and song writer," he said. "I don't

know anything about all this and never did. You seem to, so you do it."

"I got a $30-a-week raise too," Stella announced happily. "I think we ought to move."

Always cautious, I vetoed that idea for the present but knew I couldn't hold out long if Stella had made up her mind. We celebrated anyway—dinner at Schrafft's with Luxuro chocolate ice cream cake for dessert, two scoops of chocolate ice cream, almonds and chocolate sauce on spongecake. It cost 35 cents, but who cared? It was my notion of recklessness.

Afterwards we went to Gray's drugstore where we were lucky enough to get two top balcony tickets at 55 cents apiece for Mary Roberts Rinehart's *The Bat,* which we'd been wanting to see.

Downstairs at Gray's you could always get cut-rate seats for shows that had been running a long time, shows that weren't doing too well, and sometimes—on rainy nights—tickets to real hits. Courtesy of Gray's, I knew the ceilings and lighting fixtures of all the best theatres in New York.

I saw *Lightnin'* with Frank Bacon before it finally closed in New York after 1,299 performances; *A Bill of Divorcement* with young Katharine Cornell, who was much praised by the critics; Pauline Lord in Eugene O'Neill's *Anna Christie;* Laurette Taylor in a revival of *Peg O' My Heart;* Lynn Fontanne in *Dulcy;* and my favorite, Helen Hayes in *The Wren,* supported by Leslie Howard—a flop, alas!

It sounds as if I was a very discriminating theatregoer, but I wasn't. Practically anything in the way of a play filled me with rapture, and years later when I got first-night tickets regularly and often was bored, I used to think enviously of those days of easy satisfaction.

79

It would be nice to report that from this time on life was all dramatic fires, front page by-lines, promotions and raises. If life *is* like that for anybody, the person certainly isn't I. My ups are always meticulously balanced by downs and I invariably seem to go farther down than up.

One of the downs about this time (just after Stella had persuaded me to move to a more expensive apartment, too, in her favorite theatrical forties) was the return to the *Mail* of Zoë Beckley, to my mind the best woman feature writer a newspaper ever had. I'd known and admired her work, even in Missouri, but somehow never expected to see her in the flesh. When I did, it was too bad but natural that my first feeling should be one of apprehension and jealousy.

I'd been having it all my own way as the distaff member of the news and feature departments. Zoë, just back from Europe, had been a star on the *Mail* a year or so before and certainly would be again. So I was absolutely certain I'd be fired, for what use could they possibly have for me with her there?

I went through the motions of appearing every day, expecting each to be my last, but to my delighted surprise, everybody treated me as usual and my daily feature story, usually an assignment I had given myself, was printed as always.

I had started making up story assignments for myself in a week when nobody else seemed to have any ideas. That first effort got by, so I ventured to try it again. Now it seemed an extra hazard. Maybe they were just giving me enough rope to hang myself. I dreaded to meet the woman I had admired so much. She was in and out of the office, but we always seemed to miss each other until one day just as I was getting ready to leave, I saw her coming toward me.

"I'm Zoë Beckley," she said, holding out a cordial hand. "And I know you're Mary Margaret. I'm so glad you're here today for I wanted to tell you that the story you wrote about the Village yesterday is just about the best feature story I ever read."

I was so overcome that I could only blush and try to stammer my gratitude. She went right on commenting on other stories of mine which she'd read and soon she had put me completely at ease. I can honestly say that from that day on I never knew a moment's jealousy of her, though it was true that she got many of the plums that might have fallen to me if she hadn't been there—such as going to Europe to escort Lady Astor to America and later Coué and later still Queen Marie of Roumania. Though come to think of it, these were Zoë's own suggestions and she had the force and courage to put them over. Probably I'd never have dared to suggest such things even if she hadn't been there.

My Village story wasn't very good, I decided when I reread it, but I glowed with gratification for Zoë's praise. It compared life in Greenwich Village to that in Paris, Missouri; told how the obliging iceman would empty your mousetrap and reset it for you, how the grocery man once he got to know you would charge your vegetables and fruits, the butcher your meat and the drugstore man your drugs—just like Paris, Missouri.

It also told about a time when some friends of Hortense's came from out of town and wanted to see the wicked Village they had heard so much about. We took them to all the places we knew where women wore cropped hair and smocks batiked in reds, blues and greens all running to-

gether, places where long-haired poets sold sonnets and
love candy, where soulful-eyed artists sketched pictures of
diners, and gypsies told tea-leaf fortunes—but still the
visitors seemed disappointed. It wasn't until a traveling
man in one restaurant, getting more and more tipsy on
the bathtub gin he was drinking out of a teacup, lurched
over, chucked one of Hortense's friends under the chin
and leeringly called her "girlie" that they felt they'd
seen life in the raw. (Zoë laughed, remembering that.)

"It's exactly the way out-of-towners are," she said, and
I felt linked with her as an experienced urbanite.

Zoë was Irish, with black curly hair which she wore short
long before other women did. She had thick dark brows
and gray luminous eyes. There was a rumor around the
office that she scrubbed her face with Sapolio. Anyway, she
always looked as if she'd just had a bath—shiningly clean
and glowing.

All sorts of legends had grown up about her and some
of them, I guess, were true. One of the tales I checked
with her concerned the time she sat down on a park
bench beside a young man who looked shabby and
hungry. Before he knew it, they were talking together
(you *had* to talk to Zoë if she wanted you to) and he confessed that he had come to New York to try to get on the
stage. So far, he had had no luck at all and from the way he
spoke, Zoë suspected that he was thinking of suicide.

She never let on to him that she realized the depth of
his discouragement, but she took him home with her, fed
him, loaned him money for a bed and next day sent him
to a producer she knew. The producer gave the boy a
chance and before a year had passed, he was being starred
on Broadway. His name was Glenn Hunter.

Zoë had become very fond of the dynamic Queen Marie, whose sense of humor she enjoyed.

"She can laugh at herself," Zoë said after we got to be friends, and told me one of Queen Marie's stories about herself. One day she'd been having an argument with Prince Scorby, her friend and chief adviser. In order to end the argument, Prince Scorby said to her with a courtly bow, "Your Majesty, I'm glad that there is one subject we agree perfectly on: I think you're wonderful and you fully concur."

Zoë herself never acted blue but she seemed to understand and sympathize with my misgivings about myself. Stella, brisk and self-sufficient, had little patience with my anxiety about what people thought of me and she maintained that I wallowed in my worries about jobs ending. She never faced the worst until she had to and like Mr. Micawber always felt sure something would turn up. Being press agent for a song publisher suited her exactly. She met all the song writers and orchestra leaders of the time and with the blessing of Mr. Feist started taking some of them on as clients—Paul Whiteman for one, and at another time Vincent Lopez. The extra money was like a challenge and she spent it recklessly, I mournfully maintained. Not as you'd expect on clothes but on things, especially gadgets for the kitchen—trick graters, pastry tubes, reamers, strainers, meat choppers. To my dismay, most evenings she staggered in with stacks of bundles higher than her head. She never bought less than two of anything—"To have a replacement handy," she cheerily explained and added: "I don't envy anybody jewelry and furs, but when I get into the kitchen section of a store I'm putty in the hands of the clerks."

83

She collected everything—objects made of copper and silver, linen, dishes, elephants with upturned trunks. When we lived in the Village, Allen Street and its copper shops were, I've often thought, practically supported by her purchases: bowls and vases, kettles and pots.

When she was of a mind to live in an apartment, she took particular delight in cooking. She was a very good if extravagant cook. When the financial situation was right, she usually cooked about twice as much food as the company could consume. And when the mood was upon her, she was the most home-loving person I've ever known.

But after a time in an apartment, I'd notice that she was getting restless—that old winging-with-the-bluebird look would come into her eye. Usually this meant that she would soon move—into a hotel. Always she loved hotels. She liked their impersonality, I think, and she liked to be able to pick up the telephone and order meals, to have her bed made and the housework done without any more responsibility than paying for the service. And she delighted in talking to all the people: the maids, the elevator operators, the desk clerks, the hotel detective most of all.

It was really much cheaper for her to live in hotels where the temptations of the city's kitchen departments and copper shops were not so strong. During one of those hotel periods—I was living in a Village walk-up at the time—she somehow had managed to accumulate an unusual amount of extra money. When this dreadful situation revealed itself to her, she went right out and bought an automobile—a Buick sedan, shiny black with balloon tires and clutch, brake and gas-accelerator pedal specially built up so she could reach them.

As soon as the magnificent car was delivered, she telephoned and grandly invited me to go for a ride. We were proceeding up Park Avenue at a slow pace, Stella concentrating on the gear handle, finding the horn, admiring the dashboard, and I, scared to death and yelling, "Look out for that car! Stella, he's too close to you!" Suddenly, as we meandered across the 48th Street intersection, a uniformed patrolman whistled. Stella slammed on the brake and we pulled up to the curb. The officer bore down on the driver's side with an angry face.

"I'm writing you a ticket," he declared. "License and registration, please."

"What was I doing?" demanded Stella.

"You were driving too slow, that's what," asserted the policeman righteously. "Driving too slow is against the law. It blocks traffic and creates a dangerous situation."

"A ticket for driving too slow?" Stella repeated incredulously. "Is that all you cops have to do—hold up citizens who are driving carefully? Why don't you stop all these speeders? And the town is full of thieves and pickpockets!"

The officer had his ticketbook out and was preparing to write.

"Never mind," commanded Stella. "You get right into this car. We're going to your precinct station. *I'm* arresting *you*. Get in."

I knew she meant every word of it. And, envisioning a mess at the police station—visualizing both of us in jail— I immediately began to cry.

"Oh, no, Stella," I pleaded. "*Please* don't arrest the policeman. It was a misunderstanding. He's a nice man. Don't make trouble for him. Let him go!"

"No," said Stella with dangerous calm. "It is an outrage when taxpayers can be persecuted for obeying the law. I'm taking him to the police station."

By this time the policeman had completely lost his composure—even his nerve. He could see that Stella was perfectly capable of doing what she threatened and he thought about headlines and publicity that wouldn't do him any good.

"Listen, lady," he began placatingly. "I'm just doing my duty."

His first fine fury had all evaporated. He was on the defensive and Stella kept him there, ending by letting him off—only because, she told friends later, "Mary Margaret made such a scene. I ought to have taken him right to the precinct!"

7. Everybody Saw Paris

ALTHOUGH I· had desperate days, like the one on which Stella Karn ran into me on Seventh Avenue, bound for the Western Union office to telegraph my mother that I was coming home for good, I mostly reveled in every moment I spent on a New York newspaper. The crisis that day was a double-header. First, one of my stories had been butchered by a copy reader and second, I was jealous because my current beau had shown interest in another girl

—more than interest in fact. I had caught the two of them locked in a close embrace in the kitchen of a friend's house where we were having a party.

"We're just good friends," Jane had the presence of mind to assure me even as she extricated herself from Jim's arms. Jim, very red in the face, echoed feebly, "It's platonic." But he didn't expect to get away with it for he knew that I did not hold with the idea rapidly becoming popular that kisses meant nothing serious. A young man kissed me at his peril. I either slapped him or assumed he wanted to marry me.

On this occasion, Stella comforted me as usual by taking me into Schrafft's and buying me a double portion of Luxuro ice cream cake—with pecans and hot butterscotch sauce this time. As this incident proves, I never felt really secure in my love life or in my job, not for long, even when I had two beaux at once and a by-line on front page center.

So when Stella Karn suggested, after I'd been on the *Mail* about a year and a half, "Let's go to Europe this vacation," I was speechless. When I got my breath, I almost shrieked, "I couldn't go to Europe. How should I pay for it? It would take too long away. I'd lose my job."

Stella had undoubtedly anticipated my entire reaction so it did not ruffle her. She very calmly answered my objections in one astounding sentence. "I am sure you can talk Mr. Stoddard and Mr. Niles [the owner and managing editor of the *Mail*, respectively] into letting you send back stories from Europe, paying your salary and extending your time away," she assured me. Then she added the clincher: "It won't cost us anything for the passage because my mat service will pay."

Stella's mat service was a promotion feature she had

worked out for Leo Feist. She sent it free to papers all over the country and hundreds of them printed it. The advantage was that if a paper used it at all—it came complete with pictures and text—they had to use it with publicity blurbs intact. I usually wrote the stories, for while Stella could write very well when she chose, she seldom chose. Too lazy, I told her, not that I really minded, for writing that kind of thing was easy for me.

Often she combined two clients at a time in the releases —an orchestra leader, say, and a popular song. Therefore to pay for the trip would be simple. She would simply combine the steamship line of our choice with a popular song. I wrote some colorful pieces about life on shipboard and Stella got the orchestra to play "Three O'Clock in the Morning," "My Man," and all the other Feist numbers she was plugging so that my stories would be truthful. I insisted on that. I suppose that the orchestras would have played the popular Feist numbers anyway, but it gave us a pleasant sense of power to hear them and feel responsible.

Mr. Niles (Theophilus his first name was) and Mr. Stoddard reacted just as Stella had predicted. Mr. Stoddard of his own accord said it would be part of my education to see Europe, and Mr. Niles opined that I ought to do some very good reporting since I would be seeing the Old World for the first time. The reporting, I'm afraid, was not very original but at least it gave me a reason for my sightseeing. Stella, who was an inveterate investigator of ruins and monuments, claimed that the minute I landed in any foreign country I went to bed with the newest American magazine I could find and a box of American milk chocolates. It is true that sea voyages, instead of resting me as they are supposed to do, drain me—literally. I was actively seasick from the time I boarded the ship (before it even left the dock) until we were about to land a week later.

That first trip I met at the last minute a perfectly charming coffee importer and I felt mournfully that if we had just had a little more time together, something delightful might have come of it. But since then, after many crossings, I have decided that there is something in sea air and the propinquity of shipboard that promotes a kind of temporary romance known nowhere else. If you see the object in Paris or London afterwards, he never looks even remotely the way he did in tweeds pacing the deck or playing shuffleboard. And whatever had seemed to be between you has vanished.

My "dispatches" to the *Mail* dealt in detail with the wonderful food on the S.S. *France*. I didn't say that a good part of it was so new to me that even without seasickness, I wouldn't have had adventure enough in me to essay the chicken in wine, frog's legs and mussels, for instance. I remember how I looked at the whole ritual of caviar service for Stella in the cabin—the horrid little round black beads accompanied by minced onion and chopped hard-boiled egg.

We landed in Plymouth and took the train for London. The four-hour trip through the incredibly green countryside was enlivened by a strangely confidential conversation with a prominent American motion picture star who had remained glamorously secluded in her cabin during the entire crossing. Maybe the long abstention from talking loosened her tongue, but at any rate I was titillated by her frank disclosure about what seemed to be an illicit affair which she was traveling to London to pursue. "He's so handsome and so strong," she confided dreamily. My last glimpse of her was as she melted into the arms of a dashing British officer. He *did* look strong, sure enough.

Several months earlier I had bought a cheap set of Dickens, complete even to *Pickwick Papers,* much of the humor of which was too broad for me, and reread all the immortal tales. So in London I reveled in the Dickens atmosphere, going to any lengths to locate the Debtors' Prison and some of the haunts of Oliver Twist, Little Nell and my other favorites.

A must too was the Cheshire Cheese, associated with Samuel Johnson. There I devoutly ordered—and loathed —underdone mutton chops and even took a sip of bitter stout which the management said was made from Johnson's own recipe. Then I gazed admiringly at the inn's oak rafters, charred from the famous fire of 1666—or so my guidebook averred.

Several years later, lunching again at the Cheshire Cheese, I had an example of the isolation in which New Yorkers live. This time I was very sophisticatedly showing a first-timer all the sights. We happened to arrive at a crowded hour and after we were seated, the headwaiter brought over a woman alone and asked if she might share our table. My friend and I smiled, murmured a conventional how-do-you-do, then went on with our talk. But as the newcomer handled the menu I found my eyes straying to her hands. She was wearing blood-red nail polish—the first I'd ever seen.

My companion followed the direction of my gaze and looked as startled as I felt. The scarlet-fingered one caught us looking and remarked amiably, "Aren't they awful? I just got it done in Paris, where it's the latest thing." Then she said to me, "You're from New York, aren't you?" I said yes. "You live on Park Avenue, number 55," she continued confidently.

91

I could only keep nodding my head, astonished and a little ill at ease. Then came the climax: "You live on the 16th floor," she charged, and followed it up instantly with, "On New Year's Eve you had a very noisy party that lasted until five in the morning and you swept the last of the guests out with a broom."

By this time I thought I must be talking to a gypsy. Then she climaxed her revelations with, "I'm your next-door neighbor, and your party kept me awake. The elevator man told me about the broom." There were two apartments on the 16th floor—she had one and I had the other but we had to go to London to meet.

On that first trip Stella was planning a trip to the Isle of Man to see a man about a Feist song and I decided to join her. We took a tiny steamer from Blackpool that plowed through the rough, rolling, rain-drenched Irish Sea. Everybody on the ship except the crew got not just *plain* seasick but *deathly* seasick, so that we were stretched out in rows on the deck, groaning and writhing and throwing up. The cabin boys went around with hoses, washing down the decks, calmly stepping over prostrate passengers who didn't even protest when a length of rubber was pulled over their legs or a spray of water splashed on them. I'm sure at one time I passed out completely and Stella was no better off.

I couldn't even eat on the Isle of Man, especially not the trotters (pig's feet) and tripe which seemed to be the main dish. The worst of it was that I had to make the voyage back and it was the same—or even more harrowing. The only consolation was that when I got back to London I found I had lost eight pounds. I remember only one thing about the Isle of Man: just as the song says, the cats they have no tails on the Isle of Man.

High point of this first European experience was that I flew from Croydon to Paris on a two-motor Haviland plane. I'd been worried because I had heard that you were weighed publicly before the start of the flight, and in spite of the temporary loss of eight pounds I had a nightmarish fear of hearing my weight shouted from one air attendant to another. I was so relieved to find that it was only baggage that was weighed that I bore up well when the little motor roared so deafeningly that conversation was impossible and we careened as wildly as a child's toy over the choppy channel. I wasn't even sick into the little cardboard container which was thoughtfully placed in suggestively plain sight of each passenger.

My note on the channel crossing to the *Evening Mail* was, I thought, rather debonair. I wrote: "There have been one or two accidents, I believe, but in two years thousands have been carried in perfect safety. The reason more Americans get killed is that Americans are the ones who do the most flying. . . ."

Stella, indomitable sightseer that she was, took it for granted that we would view everything, complete with charabancs and guides. She asked innumerable questions and quite often set a guide straight about some event or date. She knew exactly what she wanted to look at and it wasn't always included in the regular tours, so some of her demands caused considerable anguish to the poor creatures in charge. However, they either had to produce or admit lack of knowledge. There was no other way with Stella.

She had a tender spot for Napoleon because she had read that he shared her antipathy to cats. And so when we came to his tomb, she did an even more thorough job of sightseeing than usual, determined not to miss a detail.

I impatiently went ahead and had seen all I wanted to see in much less than the allotted time. So pretty soon I walked out to wait by the charabanc for the company to reassemble. They came out in twos and threes, chattering in German, Danish, and English. We all boarded the bus. Naturally I just assumed that Stella was there, but when I looked carefully, I realized she wasn't. I saw the driver about to start and began to scream, "Wait, wait, you have left a lady behind!" At first nobody paid any attention to me and I screamed louder. The other passengers, looking at me curiously, summoned the guide, who finally, much annoyed, told the driver to pull up, then began to scold me for my friend's defection.

"She can't be there, because they were locking up just as we left," he insisted, thus increasing my agitation. I made so much noise that finally he got out, I running after him, and went back to look for Stella. Sure enough, the tomb was locked, but luckily the caretaker was right there and rather grudgingly, because he said there was nobody inside but Napoleon, he opened the doors.

There was Stella, quite contentedly and interestedly studying an inscription, oblivious to the fact that she'd caused a minor crisis and might conceivably have stayed locked in Napoleon's tomb all night. When I furiously suggested this to her, she said with complete composure, "I wouldn't have minded a bit. They don't show nearly all of it."

I have hunted vainly all over Paris to try to find again the restaurant in which I ate my first delectable dinner in that lovely city. Anyway, there never again can be such a perfect meal and perhaps my dream place would be a disillusion now. I had sole baked in almonds and cream, strawberries with Normandy clotted cream and green almonds with salt. I've had the same menu other places but it never tastes the same nor ever will, I guess.

Another of the memories that will stay with me always is arriving in Montreux, Switzerland, just before dawn and sitting on a little hotel balcony sipping hot chocolate, eating *croissants* spread with cold curls of butter and honey, just as the sun rose majestically over mountains and lake.

Another less pleasant memory is of the time I got separated from Stella on a train bound from Berne to Germany. I was put into a sleeping compartment for the night with a man. This is routine for Europe, but I didn't know that then. So I yelled as if I was being murdered. Conductors and porters came rushing, terrified that I was sick or crazy. As for the man in the compartment, he watched in open-mouthed amazement, and when I last saw him through my angry tears was shrugging his shoulders, baffled. Train attendants comforted me in three languages but I kept on yelling. At last they located Stella and made a swift exchange.

Stella had also been put in with a man but it didn't bother her. "You wouldn't be any good working for a circus," she told me, shaking her head.

It was fun back in New York to be able to say, "When I was in Paris . . ." or, "At the Cheshire Cheese in London . . ." However, it was not as good as it would be to say these things in Paris, Missouri. People in New York thought far less of crossing the ocean than the home folks did. So when the indulgent Mr. Stoddard, hearing that my mother was not well, decreed that I could have a week off to go home, it gave me my chance.

My mother was better by the time I got there, so I could devote myself without worry to the pleasures of being a minor celebrity in my home town. The Clios, a select club of women, invited me to speak at their Saturday night meeting, on my European trip and my life in New York. Here was where I got my comeuppance, as my grandmother used to call it when somebody was a little above himself and got taken down by inexorable fate.

Almost the first question asked me at the Clio meeting was "When did you last see O. O. McIntyre?" At that time O. O. McIntyre wrote a New York column which was read by literally everybody in the Middle West. Mr. McIntyre had lived in Missouri and therefore the state felt proprietary and proud of his success. He managed, as somebody writing about him said once, to wear spats and a top hat and yet maintain the attitude of the small town boy seeing the sights of the big city for the first time. It was as if he were saying to everybody back home, "You and I know this is all pretty silly and that we are the really sound people of the world—but these others are fun to talk about, aren't they?"

Naturally Miss Emma and Miss Sadie and all the other Clios thought that since I was doing so well in the big city I must now be on intimate terms with Mr. McIntyre. The truth was that I had never even seen him, except once clear across the room in a restaurant. What should I say? If I admitted that I'd never even met O. O. McIntyre, much less dined with him and held long, fascinating conversations about my work and his, they were going to think that the report of my success was pure fable. I'm not sure how I did it, but without actually lying—much—I gave a complete account of his goings and comings. I even told what he liked to eat, which was easy enough for he was always writing in his column about a certain creamy kind of rice pudding, and ice cream with chocolate sauce. My listeners had read the columns too but I made it sound as if I had shared all these delicacies with Mr. McIntyre, which I had, in a kind of way, for he was very fond of Schrafft's and I'd eaten all his favorite dishes there even if not in his company.

I got away with it, too. It was the hit of my speech, but when I was back in New York, my conscience began to trouble me—or was it really my conscience? The truth is I read in Mr. McIntyre's column that he was about to make a trip to Missouri and though I didn't know how it could be possible, I began to brood over what a horror it would be if some of those people meeting Mr. McIntyre while he was home said, "Oh, you know our Mary Margaret." And Mr. McIntyre would look at them coldly and say, "Mary Margaret? Who's she?" Finally, nerved to desperation, I wrote to Mr. McIntyre.

I began by telling him what he already knew—what a figure he was in the Middle West. Then I recounted the whole story and pleaded with him not to give me away should anybody ask about me. If I could have brought the letter back after I had mailed it I would have and certainly I didn't expect an answer. But in two days I got one, addressed in what was to become familiar to me, his clear red-penciled handwriting.

He said he understood perfectly and would take pains to spread the word in Missouri that I was doing fine, because he was sure I was. It was all as cordial and gracious as it could be. Best of all was the end. He wrote:

> I understand because the same thing happened once to me. I went home and bragged about knowing Irvin Cobb whom I admired very much but had never met. When I got back to New York, I, like you, was assailed by qualms and I did just what you've done—I wrote to Mr. Cobb and told him the whole story. He thought

97

it was a wonderful joke and we became close friends. So you see you need never worry about this again.

I've thought of it, though, many times, with gratitude to a fine generous man who understood so well a green country girl's yearning to seem important to the home folks. Later, I did meet O. O. McIntyre and his delightful wife, Maybelle. As a matter of fact, not long before his death I dined with them on good Missouri turnip greens cooked with side meat, country ham and red gravy, apple dumplings with thick cream to pour over. I even rode with the McIntyres in their famous Rolls Royce to some of the places where he gathered material for his column. I felt as if I were accompanying royalty.

Whenever I did anything—and sometimes when I hadn't—he wrote praiseful little items about me. His death was a real blow to me. I had lost a loyal friend.

8. My Conscience Bothers Me

THE combination of me and reporting in New York City was cockeyed. Especially in that reckless postwar period, to go down in history as a medley of above-the-knee skirts, cocktail shakers, moaning saxophones and general amorality. Young people in their early twenties were tagged as the Lost Generation even before the era ended.

Although I was the right age for it, I was never really

99

of it. Not that I didn't try hard to be. Many of my contemporaries, at least the ones who had experienced my kind of Calvinistic upbringing, were as torn as I was.

I had learned in the cradle about the horrors of sin and the hell fire that would punish it. I believed absolutely that right was right and wrong was wrong; that never the twain could meet.

As a young girl I wasn't allowed to learn to dance. Cards were wrong. True, our family played Authors, with pasteboards that came in suits but had author's pictures on them instead of aces, kings, queens and jacks.

I believed any number of rather horrible things would happen to you if you kissed a boy or told a lie. My mother and father never explained anything to me about sex and their avoidance of the subject made me feel that there was something shameful about human birth and the process by which it came about. Yet I was enchanted with the lambs, calves and colts I sometimes saw arrive in this world. I had a vague realization that the coming together of my father's stallion, Lyle, with the mares had something to do with colts, but I never listened to other girls when they talked about such things. Not that I wasn't interested. But I was more frightened than curious.

Vaguely I knew that something that happened between men and women was responsible for my father's refusal to let me go out alone with boys and for his always coming to get me at parties.

In my early teens, when I wasn't reading or thinking about what I was going to be when I grew up, I was brooding over my wickedness and resolving to be better. I built up a strange secret life of taboos and I felt guilty about something almost every minute of the day.

The fact that my Baptist preacher-grandfather and his

daughter, my mother, were the personification of all that was gentle, loving and fine made it impossible for me to rebel against the standards they set for me.

I felt differently about my father. I thought him often unjust to his children, inconsiderate of my mother and, although it was wicked according to my training to judge a parent, I felt that he was not as "good" as my mother and grandfather. I wanted to be like them—but I was, alas, my father's child. He was a man of extremes and I inherited his temperament. I never admitted this to myself, though. I was too busy being determined to be good: to control my trigger temper, not to let boys kiss me, to crusade against everything my grandfather believed to be wicked. Even then I knew that my father had a double standard—women, his women anyway, had to be good. Men—well, they were different.

While training and temperament pulled me in opposite directions, there developed within me a hard core of ambition, inspired and fostered by Mama and Pa, as I called my grandfather because Mama did. They saw no incompatibility between being good and wanting to amount to something in the world. I never was confident of myself in anything else, but I was sure I could write—mostly, I think, because they were certain of it.

When I went to college I was so busy working to support myself and to get in a little study now and then that I stayed pretty much in that early mold. My classmates, especially the other girls studying journalism, were as earnest and ambitious as I was. We were a serious group of young people, and I was the most serious of all, determined to live up to my family's—and my own—hopes. There was only one time when I was tempted to break out of this pattern. That was when I fell deeply in love with a

young medical student. Caution, aspiration, the protective-
ness of the young man and luck got me through this period
without my becoming, in the parlance of my world, a
fallen woman.

All these forces were still tearing at me when I came to
New York. Priggish though I was, I longed to be part of the
life I saw from a distance. I wanted to know writers and
artists, to go to first nights, be recognized at smart caba-
rets, speak with easy familiarity of famous stage folk. I
envied acquaintances who were talented and sophisticated, and felt shy and apologetic about my own crudeness
and lack of poise.

But everything about the city and its people was
strange to me—manners, customs of eating, drinking and
speaking. My real difficulty, though, was the standard of
morals. In the wicked city, nobody appeared to care about
right and wrong.

It was a long while before I could accept the gallantries
of city men as casually as they were meant. A man would
ask you to dinner night after night, and still be indifferent
to the idea of marriage. All he meant by being attentive
was that he wanted somebody to talk to and maybe kiss
now and then.

One evening an attractive young man who'd been taking
me to the theatre and even the Statue of Liberty stammered suddenly, "W-will you marry me?" As I hesitated,
pleased but surprised, he rushed on: "For a long time,
I've been trying to tell you I was married b-before and
divorced."

That was as far as he ever got. "Where I come from," I
informed him loftily, "divorce is a scandal and a disgrace!
I shall never marry a divorced man."

Yet I knew right then that one of my cousins was desperately unhappy with her husband, and that two other relatives were putting up with shocking infidelities. They wept, they prayed and they suffered, but the idea of divorce never even occurred to them.

Smoking and drinking seemed just about as bad as divorce to me. I was convinced that one cocktail led directly to the Keeley Cure. Yet most of the women among my new acquaintances smoked and drank as a matter of course. On one occasion when Hortense had a glass of wine at dinner with Max and Mike, I was terrified that she'd go home and smash Mme. Duclos' furniture. "Please, please don't drink any more," I implored her.

Talk was of the frankest—at studio parties, in offices and in the homes of friends. Men and women who knew each other only casually discussed topics I would have found difficult to mention to my brothers or my father.

"I believe in trial marriage," a slightly tipsy poet told me one night at a party. "How can you tell whether you're sexually suited otherwise?" I was too shocked to answer but in less than a minute everybody else within earshot was having something to say about trial marriage and two women in the room asserted that they'd tried it. "It certainly would have been a mistake to marry Joe," one remarked frankly, "so you see how much better it was to make sure first."

I know now that all of this was part of a rebellion against Victorian standards. Young people were cutting themselves loose from the past. They wanted freedom from the old ways and taboos. But, in the course of it, they were getting away from all the old loyalties too—religion, patriotism, monogamy. They were skeptical, analytical and frank, sometimes to the point of coarseness.

I was shocked—but fascinated, too. I often felt as if I

should leave the room during discussions but lingered inconspicuously to hear all.

The twenties were just beginning to roar, the tabloid newspaper was being born to reflect a new era and, as Frederick Lewis Allen wrote, to present American life as "a three-ring circus of sport, crime and sex."

The biggest of the tabloids began on the top floor of the *Mail* building. We all watched with interest and some skepticism. "It's all pictures," I heard our office boy say. "I like it."

"It's got too much sex," one of the rewrite men pronounced severely.

Anyway, the *Daily News* grew and grew, and pretty soon city editors of non-tabloids, under the pressure of competition, were assigning us all to cover sensational divorce trials such as the Stokes and Stillman cases, and were making a Roman holiday of the Hall-Mills murders.

I was assigned at first to the Stokes divorce trial, and got so infuriated at the accusations William E. D. Stokes kept hurling at his red-haired, kitten-faced wife Helen that I finally had to be taken off the story. Every day I was editorializing in her favor:

> Her voice so low as to be inaudible to many in the courtroom, pretty Mrs. Helen Elwood Stokes today read convincingly from the little black, leatherbound book on which she pins her hope of disproving charges against her. . . .

I wrote in one lead paragraph:

> The cruel strain of the past few days has clearly told on the pretty young wife of the elderly millionaire. . . .

In fact, I rooted so obviously for Mrs. Stokes that the "elderly millionaire's" lawyer complained to Henry Stoddard, the publisher of the *Mail*.

Another trend of the times, the recoil of the older, more conservative citizens from what was happening to the young, was embodied in a meeting I covered attended by public-spirited women—Mrs. J. P. Morgan was one and Mrs. James Roosevelt was another—who were deploring the nudity of young girls and the current cheek-to-cheek way of dancing. Preachers were inveighing against youth from the pulpit: "They have no shame, no modesty," they roared—and almost any Monday I was likely to be sent to ask a clergyman to enlarge upon his indictment of girls who drank and in general were no better than they should be.

On the other hand, when a Midwestern congressman proposed legislation making it a misdemeanor for any woman to smoke in public in the District of Columbia, I whipped up next day a series of protests from women's rights champions. The women were furious, not necessarily because they advocated women smoking but because they considered such legislation discriminatory and unfair. "Women are the most discriminated-against minority in the country," Alice Paul of the National Woman's Party told me.

What was happening I know now was that nervous men were trying to control the freedom-happy "weaker sex" by statutes before it was too late. There was one legislative bill introduced that would actually have forbidden any woman to wear a dress that displayed more than three inches of her throat. My city editor had every woman on the staff, including secretaries, up for throat-measuring and since luckily I had on a gingham dress that did display just three inches of throat, he sent me out to get a man-in-the-street opinion poll.

That was the kind of assignment I shrank from, but somehow, when it was my job, I always managed to get up the nerve to stop the more amiable-looking passers-by in front of City Hall.

Once, when I was particularly indignant about the silly subject I had to question a stranger about and got a staggering rebuff from a curmudgeon, I stopped trying and just invented my whole story. I was bored with the usual occupations—file clerk, plumber, secretary—and dreamed up a few that were more unusual.

"What on earth is a buttoner?" quizzed my perplexed city editor.

"I asked the same question," I assured him earnestly. "He's the man who comes into the shop window after the window dresser has put the dresses on the dummy. He buttons the dresses up."

The city editor accepted the explanation but went away shaking his head. It seemed a lovely joke at the time—but I worried about it once I saw the story in print. Reporters are supposed to be accurate, honest and reliable, and after all, I was planning to be one of the great ones.

That was always the way. I *wanted* to be a paragon of virtue but I wasn't. Sometimes I even fibbed when I thought it was going to be hard to get a story; that is, I represented myself as coming from *The New York Times*. I thought *nobody* would refuse a gentlewoman from the important *Times*.

Whenever I had done something my conscience tormented me for, I worked hard for the Save-A-Home Fund, which was my form of expiation. When I started on the *Mail* the Christmas season was near, and since I was a sob sister in the editor's eyes I was immediately assigned to the *Mail*'s Save-A-Home Fund. If a needy family was in danger of being evicted, contributions from the *Mail*'s readers literally saved their home. The approach of the holiday stepped up all the efforts.

The social worker in charge of investigating each case was Miss Bertha Pohlman, and I, as the reporter, attempted to stitch the tale together in about 500 heart-tugging words a day. At first I got my material secondhand from Miss P., but as time went on, because she was a little more brisk in her reports than I liked, I begged to go with her on her rounds in order to find material for myself that would make our readers turn their pockets inside out. I climbed hundreds of flights of stairs, entered dark, smelly tenements, talked to many sick and despairing women, stumbled over countless drunken men and boys.

Nobody knows how many stories I wrote through the years about hungry little children, ailing widows, deserted wives, unemployed husbands walking snowy streets in vain search for work.

One Save-A-Home Fund story I remember was about a frail woman deserted by her husband while she was in the hospital bearing his child. The brute added to his cruelty by carting away all their clothing and household equipment and selling it.

"I hate shop windows" was the lead on a story in which I told the sad plight of a woman who faced Christmas with a husband in prison, an eviction notice from the landlord, three small children and no job.

"When Peter asked why Daddy never came home, Peter's mother burst into tears" was the start of another sad tale. They were all true, too, these sagas of suffering and I felt them keenly.

Not all my verbal sobbing was confined to the Save-A-Home Fund stories. Right after I was pulled abruptly off the Stokes trial, I had a page one by-line story on the discovery of a darling little girl foundling by the fashionable bachelor rector, Percy Stickney Grant, on the doorstep of his home.

And another front-pager of mine related the arrival of 13 English war orphans on the *Aquitania* for adoption in the United States. I must have made a case for them, for though the children were already claimed for adoption, for days afterward the *Mail* was deluged with requests from sympathetic readers who wanted to take one or more of the little waifs.

The war orphan story was part of one of the most exciting experiences of a reporter: going down the bay before dawn in the customs tender to meet incoming transatlantic liners.

9. Down the Bay

ALTHOUGH it meant getting up before dawn and rushing down to the Battery on the subway filled with early-morning workers, going down the bay was my favorite assignment.

Each newspaper had a ship newsman, but whenever there was a titled person or a famous author, actor, or anybody arriving from the other side who stood out from his fellows because of position or achievements, I went down the bay in the revenue cutter that carried the customs men to quarantine.

First the health officers boarded the ship which lay at anchor, and our little cutter churned around in the bay while we waited for the flag to go up that would indicate the doctors had found no infectious disease. I used to dread the moment of climbing a rope ladder up the side of the ship. It was often windy, so that my skirts frequently blew up clear over my head. I couldn't have endured such an embarrassment if it hadn't been my job. I would go to strange men's hotel rooms, accost unknowns in the street, visit a dive if necessary, as long as it was an assignment. I would look at accidents, fire, gore and even death with comparative equanimity, as long as it was part of the day's routine. True, underneath I had the same old qualms but I subdued them successfully enough to complete my chore, whatever it was. Also, when going down the bay I wore long, all-encompassing bloomers, purple or green, especially bought on the East Side for ladder climbing.

The world is so much smaller these days than it was in the early twenties that the newspaper habit of front-paging any foreign visitor who had even slight pretensions to public interest now seems strange. Besides lords and ladies, actors and writers, Irish martyrs and those connected with them furnished material for more than one of my down-the-bay interviews.

My very first trip was to meet Mrs. Terence McSweeney, whose husband, Lord Mayor of Cork, had starved himself to death as a protest against the policy of England toward Ireland.

I didn't know a single reporter on the revenue cutter that first morning and felt dismal and scared. I'll never forget Alice Rohe (she represented United Press) who was kind enough to let me stand near her.

Mrs. McSweeney received the 30 or 40 reporters in the ship's writing room and, looking as frightened as I felt, read a statement. I took notes furiously and rushed back to the office as soon as the ship landed to write that the soul of sorrowful Ireland looked out of her blue eyes and to predict that her tour of America would be a great success.

After I turned in my story, I was assigned to cover Mrs. McSweeney during her entire New York visit and dashed away again to her headquarters in the St. Regis Hotel. There a desk clerk told me that she had left for some unspecified destination. I was frantic, for as usual I felt certain I'd be scooped and to be scooped was the most awful disgrace I could imagine. To recover my poise and get courage to pursue Mrs. McSweeney to whatever ends of the earth she might have gone, I sat down in one of the big lobby chairs and, to my horror, tears began to slip out of my eyes and down my cheeks.

Labert St. Clair, who was doing publicity for the group that had brought Mrs. McSweeney to America—The Irish Friends of Eamon de Valera—came into the lobby at this moment and quickly crossed to where I was sitting. He tells about the incident in a book he later wrote:

> I saw a young girl sitting alone in one corner of the lobby, sobbing and dabbing at her eyes with a little handkerchief. In her lap was a pad of copy paper folded three ways, so I knew she was a reporter.

Then he quotes me as telling him that I'd just that day got my job on the *Mail*. (What I probably said was that I'd gone down the bay for the first time that day.) He claims that I added sorrowfully: "Now Mrs. McSweeney's gone downtown and all the other reporters are with her. I'll be scooped and fired."

Mr. St. Clair, I must say, ran true to my experience with men. He offered me his own big handkerchief to swab away my tears and then told me the delightful news that Mrs. McSweeney was right there in the hotel, and that he would take me to her.

He records:

> The girl's sobbing soon turned to laughter. She got an exclusive story which hit the front page of her paper, and the city editor praised her.

The reason my story hit the front page was that Mrs. McSweeney told details of her husband's long fast and her own agony as she stood by and watched him slowly starving to death.

She ended the interview by saying, "My only desire now is to see that he didn't starve in vain."

It was a very good day all round for me, because I not only landed my story, I also met Bert St. Clair, who became one of my best friends.

As my confidence increased I began to make friends with many of the incoming celebrities, too.

The English viscountess, Sybil Rhondda, sailed in one day without putting her name on the passenger list and a stewardess tipped me off about her. She had come over for a holiday in Connecticut with a friend and wasn't eager to give an interview, but couldn't bear to turn down an earnest woman reporter. She was one of the early champions of the right of women to have equal pay and opportunity with men. Only a few months before, her application for a seat in the House of Lords had been turned down. I'm sorry she didn't live to read the bill signed by Queen Elizabeth II in 1958 that would have allowed her the privilege she was seeking.

I got a front page by-line on the Lady Rhondda story and an invitation from the lady herself to have lunch when I came to London. This independent woman of title was as indifferent to clothes as I. At the luncheon a few months later at her club she snatched off her hat and hung it on a clothes tree near the table, and I immediately snatched off my hat and hung it beside hers. She showed me a side of England I never could have seen without her: distinguished women working together to better the lot of children, to arouse their own sex to efforts on behalf of peace, and to improve living conditions for everybody.

Another Englishwoman who opened doors on the world for me was Maude Royden, whom I also met down the bay and saw that summer in England. She was pastor of a church in the slum section of London. I can never forget the picture she made in the pulpit—a small figure with sad dark eyes who seemed to symbolize the kind of enveloping maternal instinct you find in certain women which doesn't limit itself to one family but reaches out to all sick and oppressed.

British author E. Phillips Oppenheim—then at the peak of his popularity and a favorite of mine—explained that he didn't write much about women in his books and went light on love interest because "woman—she is utterly insoluble. I've never even tried to understand her."

Mr. Oppenheim resembled his own heroes—very British and understated in impeccable tweeds and full of dry humor. He was turning out international adventure mysteries—all very high class and glamorous—set in the *salon privé* at Monte Carlo, or British hunting lodges, and the hero was always rich, self-assured and usually titled. Carolyn Wells, who also did mystery stories but in a more down-to-earth American style, once remarked to me that Oppenheim's heroes were the only men in literature who "selected" rather than just took a cigarette from a case.

Mr. Oppenheim, who may not have understood women, was nevertheless in a big hurry to get off the ship because he had, he explained, a luncheon date with one of the attractive enigmas.

Sir Arthur Conan Doyle came to New York, not to talk about his immortal Sherlock Holmes but about spiritualism. He was beginning to confide, at first privately and then publicly, that he was sick of Sherlock and hoped very much that he would not be remembered solely as the detective's creator. He had already made efforts to kill off the master detective, which Sherlock's public all over the world had indignantly spiked, and I think the reason he and Lady Doyle talked to me as often as I requested and even invited me to visit them in England was that I didn't seem to care in the least about Sherlock and was fascinated by spiritualism.

It was spine-tingling when Sir Arthur looked me straight in the eye and said: "I have seen the face of my dead mother as plainly as I see you now. I saw her wrinkles and her eyes. . . ."

Lady Doyle declared that she was interested in converting Americans to spiritualism so that we should have happier children. She was opposed to the old idea of hell fire and brimstone and had taught her children about spiritualism as soon as they were able to talk, stressing that death is not something to be dreaded but is only walking into another and far more pleasant room.

I asked Billy, who came in when we were discussing heaven, "What do you think heaven is like?"

The little girl—her real name was Kitty but she preferred Billy because she wanted to be a boy like her two brothers—answered, "Heaven is a happy place where you do better all the things you like to do here and see the people you like. You are kind to everybody and everybody is kind to you."

The Doyles were at their country house in Sussex when I spent a rather startling day and night with them. Sir Arthur, with his worn country tweeds, rosy cheeks and broad frame warming himself before the blazing fire in a great stone fireplace, seemed to me to epitomize everything I'd ever read or heard about the English country gentleman. But instead of talking about cattle raising, hunting, and his garden, as you'd expect from his appearance, he spoke as he had in New York, of trying to convince the world of the truth of spiritualism.

In fact, the Doyles talked more about dead people than live ones, and a solid British luncheon of rare roast beef, Yorkshire pudding and Brussels sprouts was accompanied by a conversation (in which the waitress joined) about a prospective séance at which Lady Doyle hoped to get in touch with the waitress's recently dead father.

After luncheon, the children went off on concerns of their own and I sat with Lady Doyle in the library while she got automatic writing, this time from a long-departed relative of hers. Toward teatime—crumpets, jam and good strong English tea with milk—the children came running in from the garden.

"What have you been doing, darlings?" asked their mother affectionately.

They replied almost with one voice, "Oh, we've just been playing football with Kingsley."

Kingsley was Sir Arthur's son by an earlier marriage. He had been killed in World War I.

An especially huge delegation of reporters and photographers went down the bay the day the Princess Anastasia of Greece came home after her marriage a short time before to Prince Christopher of Greece, youngest brother of the reigning King Constantine. Princess Anastasia's first husband was William B. Leeds, the tin-plate king, and her courtship and second marriage had been front page headlines all over the world. *She* was the first American woman to become a royal princess.

While his wife told women reporters about being famished for a sight of home (meaning America) the prince handed out cigarettes and cracked jokes with the men reporters. My story commented on his English, but I did not know then what I was later to learn from hearing him answer questions by the hour: he spoke six languages perfectly, including Oxford English.

Of course an American woman who has married real, honest-to-goodness royalty would be a Page One story any time. But it was an even bigger story at that curious period of our history because we were still in a state of awe about titles. I remember cornering one Frenchwoman for no reason whatever except that she was a marquise, and digging out of her a ridiculous little message to the effect that it wasn't really the prospect of marrying money which was resulting in the wholesale influx of eligible European men with lesser titles, it was the international reputation of American girls for beauty.

My determined search for titles even pushed me on one

occasion into the third-class section of the *Resolute,* where I turned up the Countess Christine de Rosenkrantz arriving quietly for her first visit to the country. It turned out, however, that it was not lack of funds which put the countess below deck, but a determination to find out for herself the conditions under which her fellow countrymen were immigrating.

It was rare, however, for our distinguished visitors to travel any way but first class—and I can't remember that any of them, with one major exception, were reluctant about facing either photographers or reporters, although when memoirs came out later (which almost inevitably they did) it was the modest fashion to complain wryly about the publicity deluge.

Ship news photographers were noted for their brashness and sometimes I thought they went out of their way to maintain the legend of impudence. They addressed royalty as "Hey, prince," which didn't shock me at all, but I never quite got over the time we went down to meet the Oberammergau players, who came over from Germany to put on their famous Passion play. They were a strange and picturesque-looking lot, for they lived and dressed their parts the year round, and most of the men wore full beards and long hair. Anton Lang, a wood carver who played Christ, looked like the conventional paintings of the Master, and when you saw him in the flowing robes of the time he was portraying, it usually had a sobering effect upon even the most disrespectful.

Not, however, upon one photographer. The press was all gathered with the players on the upper deck. The reporters had had their innings and the photographers had taken over. They posed the players in groups that suggested more and more the traditional. Then one photographer got an idea. He focused his black box on Anton Lang. "Hey, J.C.," he shouted, "get up there on the rail so that we can take a picture of you walking on water."

There was a startled silence for a minute and then everybody began to talk at once. The players knew a smattering of English, but at any difficult moment it was possible for them to plead lack of understanding. So Anton Lang—either because he really did not understand or did not choose to—simply went quietly below to his cabin.

The Passion players spent Christmas in New York that year and I was assigned to follow Anton Lang along crowded Fifth Avenue on Christmas Eve. The snow was falling in soft, lazy flakes and harassed last-minute shoppers were striding ahead, eyes front, thinking of nothing but getting those last few gifts. On nearly every corner a red-robed Santa Claus was ringing a bell to call attention to his great iron kettle into which he hoped passers-by would drop coins for the Volunteers of America.

Lang, in his flowing robes, head bare, beautiful face serene, walked through the throng as if it were not there. Some, absorbed in their own concerns, missed him entirely; others suddenly turned back, startled, to take a second look as if discrediting their own eyes. I kept a few paces in back and gradually we collected a small parade, mostly children but some grownups, too, curious to see where the Christus of the Oberammergau players was going. He made a few stops, for he too was doing last-minute shopping. Two or three times, in one or another store, a woman with a child would hold the child up, and the Christus would gravely lay his hand on the child's head and kiss it on the forehead.

Before the expedition was over I was bogged down by

sentimentality—and only at this late date have I been willing to admit that the trip through the city was arranged by the company press agent. Not the response of the public, though. That at least was genuine.

10. Heroines and Murderers

ALTHOUGH she shrank from publicity as violently as most of our illustrious visitors courted it, the biggest aggregation of reporters and photographers that ever went down the bay in my time met Mme. Marie Curie, co-discoverer with her husband of radium.

Mme. Curie and her two daughters, Irene and Eve, were brought to this country by a national committee headed by Mrs. William Brown Meloney which through public subscription had raised money enough to buy a gramme of radium for the Polish scientist's research work. Mrs. Meloney, who was usually very sure of herself, was humble when it came to Marie Curie. For 20 years she tried to get an audience with the self-effacing little scientist and when she finally met her idol face to face she was shaking with emotion. That was somewhat the effect Marie Curie had upon even the most brash photographers.

Of course, she was then and has remained the great name among women in science, but that was only part of it. Everybody who saw her seemed to feel her complete integrity, her devotion to her work, her dedicated idealism. Although I only once shook her small hand, roughened and scarred by her work in the laboratory, she affected my whole life in the strangest way.

I've thought sometimes that she restored the faith I had as a child in goodness and truth. The story had preceded her of what she had replied to her husband when he explained to her that the interest in and demand for the secret of radium was becoming so great that they must make a decision as to whether they would patent it and reap a fortune beyond all imagining or give it freely to the world. The wife scarcely looked up from her test tubes as she said, "Oh, but that was decided long ago. It's not ours. It belongs to the world."

This, along with the report of the great love between the husband and wife and her inconsolable grief when he was killed in a street accident, had made her a figure of legend and dreams. Perhaps we felt that if there was even one person like her in the world, then in spite of disappointment, frustration and disillusionment, this couldn't be such a bad place.

The little figure, in its round black hat and straight

black dress with white turnover collar, looked so frail, weary and sorrowful that not the most aggressive among us tried more than perfunctorily to get her to amplify her brief denial that she had ever said that radium could cure cancer. Nobody ever got a real interview from her and the speeches she made acknowledging the dozens of honors, degrees, and medals that were bestowed on her were probably the shortest on record.

Later, in Mrs. Meloney's living room, I talked to Irene, then twenty-one, who already was more interested in science than anything else. She said: "That one must do some work seriously and must be independent and not merely amuse oneself in life—this our mother has told us always, but never that science was the only career worth following."

Eve, sixteen, called by everyone "the little one," was pretty, vivacious and grateful for the efforts made by sons and daughters of the Marie Curie Committee members to arrange a little diversion now and then for the two girls. They escaped for a few hours to Coney Island where they rode the roller coaster, ate candied apples on sticks and even sampled hot dogs. But quickly they had to return to duty. Although every effort was made to protect the mother, she finally was unable to continue the grueling routine of receiving honors and expressing gratitude; so the job was turned over to the two girls. Solemn orators spoke their prepared speeches to fresh-faced Eve about the long years of her (her mother's) hard work, thanked her for what she had done for humanity, and she answered with becoming gravity in her mother's name.

I felt—and many agreed—that it was cruel to subject the shy and fragile woman to the rigors of an American welcome, multiplied by the cities in the country that had contributed to the price of the radium. But she apparently accepted it as part of her bargain and went on until she collapsed. She insisted from the beginning that the deed of gift, which originally made her the recipient without qualifications or conditions, should be changed so that the radium would be the property of her laboratory and could never be used commercially by anybody.

She returned as she had come, on the steamship *Olympic*, and we were all there to see her off. Her cabin was filled with so many flowers you wondered that she could breathe, and with hundreds and hundreds of telegrams.

She was very weary and far from well, but she had her precious gramme of radium and undoubtedly she thought it had been worth while. I never saw her after the ship sailed that day, but her tiny, stooped, patient figure remains a landmark in my life. To this day, whenever scientists are being attacked I feel that she is being attacked and I'm fiercely on the defensive. There may be some whose aims are selfish and mercenary, but because of Mme. Curie, I'm disinclined to believe it.

I suppose some Americans joined in smothering Marie Curie with heroine worship from the same basic emotion of curiosity that the next year turned two sordid murder cases into journalistic field days: the killing of Dot King and the Hall-Mills case. Both of them were hand-made to shock me right down to the Louis heels of my new low shoes. No matter how much I saw or experienced, any test proved that I was still at core a country girl with the stern ideas of virtue which had been drilled into me. So when I had to cover stories like the murder of Dot King, girl-about-town and, in the language of Paris, Missouri, "no better than she should be," my conviction that the wages of sin is death was strengthened.

Dot King was an ex-Follies girl, extremely beautiful, possessed of assorted sugar daddies and even a gigolo upon whom she lavished the income obtained from richer friends. One morning she was discovered by her maid, lying dead on her bed, an empty bottle of chloroform nearby, a pair of men's yellow pajamas on a chair—and some $4,000 worth of jewels missing.

With other reporters, I looked over the apartment and wrote speculative little stories about this admirer and that who was questioned. The case was never solved—so many mysteries in those days were not—but to me it was clear what had happened. She had merely paid the price, just as my grandfather had warned me.

The Hall-Mills case was hand-tailored to my ideas of morality, too—a preacher, the Rev. Edward Wheeler Hall, and the choir leader in his church, Mrs. James Mills, with whom he was supposed to have been carrying on, were found shot to death, their wicked doings exposed, their bodies laid side by side near a crabapple tree in De Russey's Lane outside New Brunswick, New Jersey.

I was part of a major journalistic exodus to Jersey, but stories that I'd done in Europe were still running under my by-line so after the first day or two at the scene I was much to my disappointment taken off the story.

It was reluctance to face the facts of life, I suppose, but I was glad on the whole that on the *Mail* my editors were never very eager to have me cover sordid trials. They preferred to send me on stories about good women, the ones who made fine wives and mothers, the kind who devoted themselves to causes, or those who because of merit occasionally reached high places or at worst had done some whimsical, feminine thing. Like the Brooklyn housewife, a violent fan of the great Babe Ruth, who finally managed to save enough money to see her idol play at Yankee Stadium. Shortly after the game started—and before the Babe had even been up to bat once—she was hit on the chest by a foul ball and knocked unconscious. Just as the hastily summoned physician ordered attendants to carry her out, she came to, realized what was happening and refused to leave. She stayed—and had the glorious triumph of seeing Babe Ruth knock a homer right out of the ball park. My story about her and her dazed rapture made Page One.

Then there was Harriet Luella McCollum, psychologist, who took one look at me and announced, "You're stingy. Your ears give you away. The lobes are small, a sure sign of stinginess." Then she went on to explain how every person can be read like an open book—that dimples, for instance, were a sign "you like to be petted." I confessed in print to my ear lobes, but took pains to point out I lacked dimples.

Any week at all I could keep the old argument going about women and careers with, for example, rich social leader Mrs. Robert Goelet saying one day that women should serve in the House and Senate, and Zoë Akin, playwright and author, averring the very next day, "A career for a woman is tragic: women are not fitted for careers—I who have one say it."

I was not much at noticing clothes, but I couldn't help myself the day Cecile Sorel, famed Parisian actress, assured me, "The secret of charm is intelligence. The secret of being loved is to be intelligent. External beauty—dimples, smiles, curls—they are nothing!" I could hardly keep my eyes off her carefully curled hair, ravishing smile and dimples, all set off by ropes and ropes of pearls and an emerald the size of a plum.

The great Lillian Russell, then almost sixty, long past the days of glory when she and Jim Brady caused a sensation in any restaurant, was an impressive figure too the morning she sailed on the S.S. *George Washington*, bound on official business for Secretary of Labor Davis. U. S. Immigration Inspector was her official title and she wore a great black picture hat wreathed with bird of paradise plumes, a blue cloth frock with flowing red sleeves, a chinchilla coat and a corsage of orchids.

She told me that she was going to Europe to get to the heart of the immigration question. "I intend to find out why immigrants who have staked all their hopes on reaching America are allowed to start on a fruitless journey," she said, referring to a scandal about dishonest men promising entrance to America, taking money and failing to deliver.

A courtly elderly gentleman came through the crowd of reporters. "You grow more beautiful every year," he said to Lillian Russell.

"I look happy, anyway," she returned, which I took for a compliment to her publisher husband, Alexander P. Moore, who later became U. S. Ambassador to Spain.

Among other women rated by the *Mail* as interesting enough for me to interview was Edith Cavanaugh of Brooklyn, who said that even though her son Freddy had gotten a broken nose boxing, she was glad she had trained him to be a boxer. And train him she did with a special punch of her very own. "To get anywhere, a boxer must have clean, regular habits and abstain from anything that tends to degrade. Otherwise his muscles will be flabby and his punch a flivver," she explained to me. So in her living room, punching bags and boxing gloves had places right beside the piano.

Vincent Richards' mother, too, believed in sports for boys. Besides Vincent, the tennis player, she had two track stars in her family. "Feed them well and teach them how ,to laugh and to play fair," she gave as her recipe for raising champions.

I sometimes interviewed champions as well as their mothers, but far from talkative was Helen Wills, who at sixteen rated as the second-best woman tennis player in the country and the youngest girl ever entered in a national tournament. Her mother was always along as chaperone and the girl was still going to bed at 9 o'clock except on an occasional dance night which always had to be Saturday.

I was on the spot when Mrs. George W. Loft got her appointment as Honorary Deputy Police Commissioner, the first time such a job, even honorary, had been bestowed on a woman. She immediately began a crusade for a second chance for the girl who has made a single misstep, this being considered a more delicate way to speak of an unwed mother—or sometimes we referred to her as one who had "gotten herself into trouble." Mrs. Loft admitted that she would have to give up a great deal to undertake her chosen work but added, "If I can do any good for any girl or woman, it will all be worth while."

In spite of flaming youth, bootleggers, bathtub gin and speakeasies, girls were still being careful where they smoked cigarettes and no magazine would show an advertisement with a woman smoking. As a matter of fact, I once saw a near riot because a girl in knee-length skirts, rouged lips and short hair walked down Fifth Avenue with a cigarette between her lips. In no time she had gathered a crowd who followed her, many crying aloud the kind of girl they thought she probably was. She finished her cigarette but apparently had had enough of smoking after that, for she failed to light another.

"She didn't know how to smoke anyway," I heard a man who had been an interested bystander remark, and I thought there was relief in his voice. Women might be doing all sorts of things that had once been marked for men only, but most men considered comfortably that they did them badly.

11. Even in New York You Have to Have Friends

ONE of my best pieces of luck was the friends I made right at the beginning of my life in New York—all people who cared more for me, I verily believe, when I was down than when I was up. That is not a typical New York habit. Stella and Hortense were the most important and next came Berta and Elmer. People who don't know the Haders regard them as figments of my imagination when I describe them and the pink stone house they built with their own hands on a hill overlooking the Hudson.

The house itself is hard enough to credit, rising as it does right out of the earth as if it had always been there. But even more fantastic is the fact that these two people who are certainly not rich went to the trouble and expense of putting in five bedrooms and almost as many baths just for their friends.

When I first knew the Haders they lived right on the river in a frame structure across the road from the site of the home they were building. The big living room had windows on the Hudson, and all the way around underneath the windows Elmer had built couches so that when 15 or 20 of us came for the weekend it served as a dormitory for either men or women depending on which sex predominated. The minority group crammed into a series of small bedrooms on various levels going down to the riverbank.

There was only one bathroom and mornings we stood in line on the stairway, toothbrushes and towels in hand, exchanging persiflage as we waited.

The Haders were struggling young artists, and like the rest of us, their periods of prosperity alternated with times of being flat broke. How they fed that mob weekend after weekend I'll never know. Everybody brought something, but the feckless were just as likely to turn up with boxes of candy or elaborate pastries which were no answer to the meat and vegetable problem.

Stella Karn was one of the sensible few who usually came with a ham or a leg of lamb. Berta had a repertoire of one-dish meals and great casseroles of Mexican earthenware in which to cook them. We ate *gnocchi*—a nourishing compound of cornmeal and cheese—great steaming caldrons of fish and meat soups, stews, baked beans seasoned with a little bit of salt pork, macaroni and spaghetti in all their forms.

We used to take the jerky little Erie train almost every Saturday afternoon after work was ended (we had a six-day week, of course), get out at the small station of Grandview and walk down the rocky hill. We were young and a little homesick, I guess, so that Berta, although she wasn't any older than we were, substituted for the mothers we were missing.

On good weekends and even rainy ones—for who cared if he got wet?—we walked miles around the countryside, now and then paired off when some random attraction drew one special man and girl together. In those days when we were so young that nobody cared very much about privacy, it was understood that we were always welcome, even without invitation. The same went for Christmas, Thanksgiving, and other family holidays. At such gatherings there often were as many as 35 or 40, for some of us brought along friends who were without ties in the big city. Berta, a saint if ever there was one, welcomed all who came. And many was the wearisome trip she made through the years on bus or train, to assuage the grief or nurse to health one of her big brood.

On almost my first visit to the Haders I saw the miniature model of their dream house, the home they hoped to build for themselves. Soon afterwards they told us that they had bought the site high on a hill overlooking the river.

When they found it, the hillside was a jungle. They had to cut their way through a mass of blackberry brambles to find out what was actually there. As they gained the top, they discovered to their delight the source of a spring and the remains of an old quarry. The spring had long ago furnished half the countryside with water during a drought. The old quarry had supplied material for many of the brownstone fronts in New York City.

The Haders began at once to dig and clear away. Every weekend we all trooped up to "help," climbing like mountain goats and looking dubiously at the prospect. Near the spring, the Haders found a pile of red rock and laid the foundation around this pile. They also used the stone for building, along with more rock dug out of the hill.

The laying of the foundation took weeks because they had to figure how to save as many trees as possible—elms, birches, sassafrass and tulip trees. They made a jut in the plan for their studio so as not to sacrifice a wide-spreading pignut tree. I sometimes accuse Berta of loving trees and animals more than humans.

After the Haders poured the concrete for the foundation, they had to stop and do some drawings to make money to go ahead. When we came for weekends now, we all dug and slashed down underbrush. Many people claim to have had a hand in the building of Hader House. When anybody asks me about my part in it, I say that I made the fudge that gave the workers quick energy to go on.

Most of the men, and women too, actually did help with the building and it was not unusual to see a girl in overalls (though overalled girls were uncommon at the time) perched on top of the roof—after there *was* a roof of course. Almost the first thing the Haders made was the great fireplace for the living room—nine feet across and big enough for a six-foot log. Then the living room was built around the fireplace. Here the Haders needed a little outside help, so they called in a neighbor and his seven sons to get the girders and beams in place. The girders of white wood, 14 x 14, were drawn up the steep hill by six horses and put into place in the ceilings and walls by the Haders and their helpers, along with the 8 x 8 chestnut beams which they support.

The two-story 38-foot-long studio has a 30-foot ceiling and a peaked roof. The glassed-in northern end is built up into a platform overlooking the gardens and here the Haders have set up their drawing boards. The platform also becomes a stage with a hanging balcony at the other end for the audience.

Hader House has features you never see anywhere else: brick walls with pockets out of which bloom Canterbury bells, petunias and lemon day lilies; birdhouses built into the house walls; a fountain in the living room; fireplaces and fountains on the terraces.

Luncheon on the front terrace with a view of the river through the trees allows the lunchers to watch the doings of a wren family which lives every year in the smallest mulberry tree. Chipmunks, gray squirrels and innumerable sparrows, cardinals, bluebirds and starlings are a part of the Hader family circle. Starlings fly in the windows and I found a friendly chipmunk once sitting spang in the middle of a warm mulberry pie on the kitchen table. A family of grackles comes back yearly to nest in the chimney and raise two families before they fly south in the fall.

Once I shared a bedroom with an orphaned gray squirrel. Another time I woke up to find it raining hard, but when I looked out the window there on the river terrace was Berta in her dressing gown, an umbrella over her head, anxiously peering up at the wrens' nest in the mulberry tree. I could hear an agitated twittering.

"They're in terrible trouble," my hostess explained

worriedly. "A strange wren has just poked his head in the nest and thrown out one of the babies."

She held the shivering bird in her hand and carefully put it back into the nest. As soon as she came inside, the mischief-making wren showed up again and this time threw four babies out on the wet grass. Berta decided it was a triangle in wren land and that the jealous suitor was trying to get rid of the babies.

Next day the father wren was discovered on the ground, hurt and unable to fly. Berta suspected he had been fighting with his rival. All the time we were having lunch on the terrace, he hopped feebly about. In the tree above, his mate encouraged him with plaintive tweets. He tried to reach her but each time fell back. Berta was crying by now and partly to quiet her and partly to help Father Wren, Elmer cut down a wild cherry tree upon which the bird could climb. The two wrens had a joyous reunion but later in the day the male was missing again and we saw him no more. Since the interloper too disappeared, we decided that perhaps they had dueled to the death.

Another time the Haders discovered a baby phoebe in the last stages of malnutrition and brought it inside to nurse it. Berta is an expert at constructing imitation worms of strips of raw beef with hard-boiled egg yolk and olive-oil heads. The phoebe grew to believe that Berta and Elmer were its parents, had the run of the house, arrived regularly for meals, and always strolled inside at dusk to spend the night. When it was old enough and fully recovered, the Haders had to put screens on the windows so that the bird would be forced to learn how to spend the night outside in his own world.

Once there was a pet robin—also rescued from death— who used to perch on Elmer's shoulder or head when he was digging in the garden and dive for the worms Elmer's spade turned up.

Berta's shopping lists take into consideration not only the people who will be her guests, but also the animals and birds to which she furnishes free board. She buys special meat for a family of raccoons who drop by the back door each night for handouts, and for groundhogs and squirrels. She also supplies the birds with a special formula containing sunflower seeds, which she orders by the 100-pound bag.

The guests at Hader House in the twenties were mainly struggling writers and artists. Berta and Elmer, though they didn't know it then, were to become top-flight authors and illustrators of children's books, many of which have included their own adventures with the birds and animals they saved from disaster.

Hader House is filled with pieces of sculpture, paintings, old tapestries, brasses and bronzes that their traveling friends have brought back from many lands. They go very well with the solid chestnut refectory tables and benches that Elmer himself carved out.

There is one drawback to having a house such as the Haders'. Soon after it was built—not finished, for although Elmer has taken the roof off six times, it is not yet finished to the Haders' satisfaction—an inspecting assessor said that it was more like a church or museum than a home and threatened to levy taxes accordingly.

Most of the regulars at Hader House came from San Francisco. For the longest time I thought I detested the place, though I'd never been there. That was because everybody I knew loved it so much and constantly bragged on it—Stella, the Haders, the Partons, the Irwins.

It's interesting to me to look back at the people who

made the greatest impression upon me in life. Half the time they probably have no idea what they've meant to me—Mary Field Parton, for instance. I was impressed by Mary's background—she was brought up a Quaker, worked in Hull House with Jane Addams, was a friend of Clarence Darrow, the famous criminal lawyer and crusader.

Mary, who was married to Lemuel Parton, newspaperman, was a crusader, too. So was Lem. They led the line of battle many times for the underdog. They lived in a little white house on the Hudson built 200 years ago by the head hay man of a great estate. It had low ceilings, small-paned windows, gabled roof, and doorsills worn down by many feet. Across from it still stands the great house, with double doors and holes in the wall that breech loaders were poked through in revolutionary days. It was in this section that George Washington threw up gun mounts to shoot across the river after the Tories took Dobbs Ferry—only it was too far for the shots to reach. Washington, in his carriage drawn by white horses, stopped at the great house with Martha on the way to Tappan nearby for the trial of André the traitor.

The flagstone terrace underneath the Parton's old grape arbor was their outdoor living room. Nearby was a meadow that was once a hunting ground for Indians. The box hedge was set out more than 200 years ago as part of a maze, but the practical farmers who succeeded the Dutch gentleman planters plowed it under as a nuisance.

I used to follow Mary from one tiny, irregularly shaped room to another as she went about her work, for I loved to hear her stories. Her brown eyes would crackle with excitement and sometimes anger as she talked about the times in Chicago when she had taken part in demonstrations against injustice.

Carl Sandburg, the poet, with his guitar and great store of folk songs, also Burl Ives singing about the rock-candy mountain, were two I met at Mary's; and it was there, also, that I first saw Inez Haynes Irwin, incredibly prolific novelist who turned out as many as three novels in a year.

Inez was married to Will Irwin, who had covered the first world war for the *Saturday Evening Post*. I suppose I've never had a more exciting moment than when Inez, with characteristic enthusiasm and hospitality, invited Stella and me to dine at 240 West 11th Street, their four-story brick house filled with old silver and glass and early-American furniture.

After the first time, Sunday night supper at the Irwins became an institution. And when they had big teas in the afternoon I was one of their regular "floaters." This meant that I went about briskly seeing that everybody had what he wanted to eat and drink, that nobody was alone in a corner, that everybody knew everybody else.

One Sunday afternoon when I was floating and feeling quite pleased with myself I pounced with glee upon two distinguished novelists and introduced Miss Fannie Hurst and Miss Edna Ferber. There were only about three things wrong with my introduction. One: they knew each other very well indeed. Two: I introduced Miss Hurst as Miss Ferber and vice versa. Three: Somebody told me when the party was over that they were having a feud. (Fannie tells me this was untrue, though sometimes they both were a trifle annoyed at being congratulated on the other's best-seller.)

I felt very foolish but Inez's loyalty never faltered. The

very next party I was again invited to float. There were always distinguished guests for Sunday night supper too— writers, actors, poets and artists. One night, at the Irwin table set with coin silver spoons and Stiegel glass, I heard from Will Irwin's own lips the story of one of the greatest feats of journalism—the way he covered the San Francisco earthquake for the New York *Sun* without leaving New York City.

Will had come on from California to work on the *Sun* and had made a fine record as a reporter. At the time of the California disaster he had just taken another job, but he dashed back to the *Sun* and announced to Chester Lord, managing editor, that he was ready to leave for the Coast.

"No," said Chester Lord, "there isn't time. You're going to write your story here." And then he explained that they'd had no word from their Coast correspondent who they now feared must be injured or dead. The journey to the Coast would require four days. So the *Sun* would get all the news possible from the government in Washington and from small-town correspondents near San Francisco— and for the rest, Will Irwin, who knew San Francisco as he knew his mother's face, would write the story. He would sit in the *Sun* office in New York and describe the ruin of his beloved city, vivid memory pieced out by the news that came in.

So Bill began to write—in longhand. Between that moment and deadline that day he turned out 14 columns of copy. "I could see the water front, Telegraph Hill, the hills, all spread out before me," he told me.

He kept writing at the rate of not less than eight columns a day for seven more endless days. He could never explain how he was able to go on and on, but he quoted William James, who held that we have within us a reservoir of reserve consciousness that we can call upon in times of intense-enough strain.

"And I did," Bill would always end.

The second night he went to the old Parker House for a Turkish bath and when he saw women in the lobby dressed in hoop skirts and bustles and men in side whiskers and choker collars, the weary Irwin began to feel sure he had lost his mind.

Just in time a bellboy reminded him that a fancy dress ball was being held, and a little reassured, he plunged into the Turkish bath and then dashed back to the office. In the intervals of work he worried about the fate of his family in San Francisco until a friend got a telegram through that said they were safe. That gave him new strength.

I made Bill tell the story over and over and always cheered when he added that after it was all ended and the results totted up, the *Sun* had come out better than many of the papers that had printed eye-witness reports. Bill really knew his San Francisco.

Another of my favorite Irwin stories was about the time he got assigned by *Collier's* magazine to track down phony mediums all over the country. Sometimes he visited séances as a client, but it wasn't until he knew enough of the patter of the trade to pass himself off as Professor Beach, the great California clairvoyant, that he began to uncover really exciting material for his article.

To get it he acted as helper for a while to a woman medium whom he called Martha. He moved from his hotel to a furnished room, cut every mark of identification out of his clothes and reported to Martha. It was chilly and all the customers wore coats. These Martha hung on a rack in the hall. Bill asked each sitter to place a personal object on the table and chatted for long enough for Martha to go through the pockets of the coats in the hall for letters, cards and any object that might prove useful for identification. On a sheet of paper she would put down brief notes, such as "red dress—rear front, from Peoria. Agnes, bad cough, family in drugs, Johnny, Joe."

When she came in to give her little introductory talk she dropped the paper tightly folded among the objects on the table. Bill, fumbling among them "to get the aura," palmed the paper, retreated to the hall, memorized the notes, and came back for a demonstration of spirit power.

Eventually Martha gave Bill the information he wanted about the Blue Book mediums in Chicago, who kept a card-index system of regular visitors. As soon as a medium learned the name of a sitter, she would telephone the Blue Book and the files would provide perfect information for a demonstration.

This story inspired me to suggest to our city editor that I visit a few mediums to see what I could unearth. The first one refused me entirely on the ground that I was too skeptical. Maybe she saw my pencil sticking out somewhere. The next two charged $2 apiece and seemed to have regulars who groaned and moaned as if they were getting messages from the other world. Nothing came for me, but a very strange thing happened at the next place.

It was up three flights of stairs, in a dark little apartment with a few old people sitting round, holding hands while we sang "Rock of Ages." The medium seemed to go into a trance—the others had merely talked sociably with the patrons. When the lights were out, a squeaky little girl's voice came from where Madam Astra was sitting. She gave messages to various women and then she said,

"I see a letter from somebody named Elizabeth. You love this woman very much and she is sick—very sick."

Remembering Bill's stories, I had been careful never to leave my bag or coat where anybody could get at it. But in my bag at that moment was a letter from my mother, whose name was Elizabeth. Only it was signed Mother, and not Elizabeth, and she didn't say she was very sick—just that she hadn't been feeling well for several days.

The experience frightened me. I rushed to a telephone to call my mother (she was feeling better) and next day I told my city editor that I thought, after all, I'd give up the story about mediums.

Surrounded as I was by inveterate hostesses—Berta, Inez, Mary Parton, especially Stella—I remained the reluctant partygoer and even more reluctant hostess. But when Stella and I shared an apartment, I had no choice.

Stella adored parties. She loved big aggregations of people. I've seen her in the middle of some really important negotiations with lawyers, advertising agency executives or broadcasting network heads, briskly wind up the conference pleading a pressing engagement. Then she'd skip off merrily to some ridiculous function: a press agent introducing a new brassière with a floor show or a toy manufacturer celebrating Christmas in July with turkey and a tree.

She'd travel miles by train, taxi or if necessary by camel to turn up at a friend's party. And she always had a fine time. But better than going to parties was giving them, the bigger the happier. On one occasion after we had moved to Park Avenue, Annette, a San Francisco friend of hers, burst in with the news that she had finally decided to marry John. If there was one thing Stella was sentimental about it was weddings. She beamed delightedly at Annette's news, announced that of course Annette and John would have their reception at our apartment, and promised to make all the necessary arrangements for the church service.

Annette, listening, began to look more and more stricken. When Stella decided where she would buy her wedding dress—white satin, of course, with orange blossoms, tulle and all the fixings (Stella knew a nice little woman who would give it to Annette wholesale) —the bride began to panic.

"Stella, no!" she pleaded. "John and I are just going to slip off quietly next week and get married in Connecticut. After all, we've been living together for three years and *everybody* knows it. I'd feel such a fool. I don't want a reception! Please, Stella. . . ."

Stella went on with her plans as if she hadn't heard. John, coming by to get Annette for dinner, agreed enthusiastically about everything. By that time Annette was ready to cry.

"If I had my way," she bitterly informed her fiancé, "I'd make you marry Stella in Grand Central Palace with thousands to watch."

Annette won about the quiet wedding, but Stella had the reception at our apartment, with a hundred guests and the best chicken salad I ever ate—hunks of white meat, toasted almonds and white grapes with a cream and mayonnaise dressing from a little catering place in the Village.

Stella collected for parties the way a painting connoisseur gathers canvases. She had a list of off-beat specialties and an even longer list of off-beat people. Then, when a party was in the offing, she would make up the menu and the guest list and "dress" the gala the way a good theatre manager arranges the seating of a first night so as to show off his distinguished audience to best advantage.

One of her favorite devices was a sprinkling of titles. Somewhere she had run across Don Jaime, a younger son of King Alfonso of Spain, and he turned up—dark, smooth and distinguished—at a number of Stella's gatherings. So did a prince whose name I've forgotten, and Lady Moira Bathurst, whom I first met at dinner at Elizabeth Marbury's. Stella, who never was very good at names (although she never forgot a title), usually called her Lady Bathtub.

She also pulled in a sampling of famous names from show business, circus and carnival; writers, playwrights, songwriters. It was often a curious mélange, but somehow her parties went off marvelously. I stayed in the background, grumbling because the place was going to be a mess. Stella never paid any attention to objections of any kind once she made up her mind.

Inez Irwin—an indefatigable party-giver herself—was Stella's greatest admirer. It was like Sarah Bernhardt complimenting Eleonora Duse when Inez, her face alight, would look admiringly over Stella's merry throng and murmur, "She's a second Mrs. Stuyvesant Fish, that's what she is, a second Mrs. Stuyvesant Fish!" (Mrs. Fish was the one who gave the hundred-thousand-dollar soirees at Newport.)

Vasiliu

12. Nonsense Era

FOR days and even weeks at a time, everything I did either for the paper or as amusement in my free hours seemed to me deliciously absurd. It was indeed a wacky period. People trying to shake off the memory of a frightening war were like children who wouldn't take a dare from anybody.

I was always covering contests, either of endurance or skill. The Connecticut owner of a cow claimed that his

Bessy would give more milk than any other cow and richer milk, too. A woman in New Jersey offered to match a hen named Lottie against any other hen in the world for egg production. Everybody wanted to have the biggest—pumpkins, tomatoes, cabbage heads. It reminded me of the county fair back home when whole neighborhoods got involved in such contests and in a little while nobody was speaking to anybody else.

One of my most nauseating assignments was to watch two men eat raw oysters. The winner downed over a hundred with Tabasco sauce. He was very sick right afterwards, and so was I. Sometimes it was a pie-eater who challenged other pie-eaters, or a woodchopper or a knottier.

One woman claimed she could knit an afghan faster than any afghan had ever been knitted before. Another anticipated mixes by making a cake from scratch in seven minutes. If it wasn't an individual it was an organization throwing out a challenge. I interviewed more mothers of healthiest babies than a pediatrician; listened to more amateur talent than a booking agent.

The ultimate in absurdity came along later with flagpole sitting and marathon dancing. Otherwise quite sane people were fascinated by these spectacles. Men and women would stand for hours gawking up at a fellow human perched on a tiny platform on top of a long stick. Nothing ever happened except the raising and lowering of food in pails or an occasional exchange of persiflage between the sitter and a friend on the ground. However, hope sprang eternal. He might faint up there; he might go to sleep and fall off. He might even decide to come down and what a triumph to say you were there when the flagpole sitter either broke a record or gave up trying.

I had one experience of modified flagpole sitting myself. The assignment came from Mr. Stoddard. Traffic towers had been erected along Fifth Avenue as an experiment. The increasing number of automobiles had made some sort of control necessary. Each tower contained a policeman to turn the lights from red to green and Mr. Stoddard suggested that I sit in the one at 42nd Street for a few hours.

Motorists looking up were startled to see me busily making notes, and before the day was over, friends who had learned of my temporary elevation found reason to stroll by and engage in gay banter from the sidewalk. I shared the policeman's noonday sandwiches and for my piece drew all sorts of conclusions about the manners and morals of the motoring public. I was just as glad, however, that it was a one-day assignment, for the quarters were cramped to say the least—not more than a few inches leeway whichever direction you turned and I kept bumping my head on the top of the tower.

The marathon dancers who dragged themselves for days around stuffy, airless halls did it partly for money and partly for glory. I remember one gaunt young man who said he had been hungry for two weeks before he got the job. The couples didn't have to be very good dancers because except right at the beginning, when most of them tried to cut a few capers to impress the audience, all they had to do was cling to each other to keep from dropping in their tracks, and move their feet lethargically. The only time they brightened was when a photographer came along or when somebody from the crowd offered a fee for a special exhibition. It seems incredible, but a producer made a fortune out of that particular craze.

Perhaps naturally enough after the interval of war anxiety and fright, the eternal search for the fountain of youth was accelerated. Not-too-reputable publications were full of nostrums that purported to restore virility, eliminate lines and wrinkles—in short, stave off the onrush of time. Recipes that included lizard oil, an essence of snakeskin and the water off boiled toads were samples of some of the remedies for age.

I was actually sent all the way to Brooklyn to interview an obscure stationery store proprietor on his secret formula for everlasting youth. "Keep jolly," he urged.

I tried to get Gertrude Atherton, author of *Black Oxen*, to admit that she had taken an X-ray treatment of the glands, such as was described in her book. She was willing enough to talk about Viennese doctor Steinach's treatment which she said several friends of hers had undergone, but she evaded any personal confession. I was at a loss because I didn't know how old she was and so I couldn't tell whether she looked younger than she should have. Certainly she was a very handsome, healthy woman with red hair and vitality. Also, she seemed annoyed that women weren't flocking to Dr. Steinach. She called his method "this simple, painless miracle."

Home-coming explorers, full of tall tales of far places, added to my chronicles of the era of pleasant nonsense. One such told me of a fish he'd met that climbed trees. I didn't believe him then but I enjoyed his stories and later I found he was telling the truth. A returning naturalist described graphically a meal of termites he'd enjoyed in Africa. "You hold the live insect between your thumb and forefinger and bite it before it bites you," he explained, obviously enjoying my expression of revulsion. Pretty soon I had, from travelers I met, a whole collection of foods I hoped never to be hungry enough to try—fried caterpillars, smoked rattlesnake, whale steak, blubber, hedgehog stew.

The chroniclers of the South Sea Islands were the ones who made me feel most dissatisfied, with their talk of beautiful girls, fragrant flowers and all the food anybody could want growing right on trees and falling off in your hand without even the bother of picking. One of our reporters, who didn't care much about work anyway, had the South Sea Islands as his goal forever after one of my stories about that idyllic-sounding place.

When spring came I was frequently sent to investigate tales of animals born with two heads, birds that took care of other birds, and skunks that adopted human families and never, never used their defense mechanisms on their friends. Most of these stories didn't stand up very well but there was one source of animal sagas who always had proof of his stories—Albert Payson Terhune, author of many books about dogs. He was in but not really part of the nonsense era, for he was a solid and beloved writer with readers all over the world.

The first time I went to Sunnybank, the Terhune's home at Pompton Lakes, New Jersey, I came back with a wonderful tale of a high-bred collie that had saved a mongrel pup's life. The silly pup had strayed into the path of a train and Wolf, the collie, passing the scene, had rushed onto the tracks and pushed the little dog to safety. But he died a hero's death. The train killed him.

I stood by Wolf's grave at Sunnybank with the scent of roses and honeysuckle in my nostrils and listened to Albert Payson Terhune tell Wolf's story. Then he took me on a tour of the kennels.

The hospitable Terhunes always had something interesting to offer and I went back to Sunnybank often, frequently staying for meals that were always different from the Greenwich Village fare I ate habitually. As a special treat once they had pheasant and wild rice for me, my first taste of either. I loathed every mouthful but kept on swallowing valiantly and the wonderful ice cream and cake dessert with chocolate sauce consoled me.

Though the Master and Mistress of the Place (that's the way Albert Payson Terhune always put it in his stories) loved all their dogs, living or dead, Lad was the one they most often and most adoringly mentioned. Lad had been a house dog, and once when they thought the Mistress was dying, he had lain outside her door for 20 days without food and almost without water until she was on the road back to health. Mr. Terhune was full of yarns about him and gave me goose pimples by showing me the niche under the grand piano that had been Lad's special cave, and the space on the dining room floor where he had always lain during meals.

"Since the day of Lad's funeral," asserted the author, "no dog will ever come near either of those places." And sure enough, then and there, he ordered the current house dogs to the specified spots and each, though accustomed to rigid obedience, made wide circles to avoid Lad's province.

When I began to do better financially on the *Mail*, I moved to the third floor of an old brick house on St. Luke's Place in Greenwich Village, just opposite a children's playground that had once been a graveyard. My neighbor two doors down was Mayor Jimmy Walker, who added considerably to the gaiety of New York at that time. If I happened to be out late enough, he and I might arrive home at about the same hour. Now and then, too, I would see him earlier at one of the night spots he frequented and which I visited only when Stella made me—because they were clients—or when a beau with a walletful of admittance cards persuaded me to have a speakeasy meal.

The speakeasies had tiny barred windows in the entrance doors through which faces peered cautiously to identify you. The real men-about-town were proud of the fact that they were so well known they never had to show their cards. These dark haunts were all airless and I never could breathe in them and would frequently have to go out the heavily guarded door and stand for a while in the street.

Stella was fond of Texas Guinan, a hearty blonde with a carrying voice who, in her club, constantly exhorted her customers, whom she called "butter-and-egg men," to "give that little girl [meaning one of her performers] a great big hand." The butter-and-egg men were enchanted with her bluffness and occasional rudeness. They actually enjoyed being called suckers and at Texas' behest would get up and lumber around the floor with one of the entertainers or even attempt to sing or dance solo if she decreed it. With their antics and their teacups filled with bathtub gin, they were like actors in a comic opera or children playing tea party. I learned to shimmy at Texas' club and nearly died of embarrassment because I was so clumsy. My feet apparently remembered that Mama and Pa had taught me dancing was wicked. One of Texas' young men shoved me round the floor shaking me to make me shimmy as if he were a dog and I a toy doll. "Now, shimmy! Now, shimmy!" he kept ordering fiercely. I was not surprised, though further humiliated, when I saw him after he finished with me, whispering urgently to Texas and looking grim. Texas glanced at me, laughed a little, patted him on the shoulder and nodded. That was the end of my shimmying even when Stella offered to get her friend,

Gilda Gray, the mistress of shimmy, to finish me off. I said I was already finished.

Another night spot which Stella sometimes took me to was Casa Lopez, for Vincent Lopez, too, was a client. One of the worst moments of my life was my first time at that establishment when a waiter who had been behaving rather oddly, spilling food, breaking dishes and addressing customers too familiarly, reached under our table, right under me, in fact, and pulled out a woman's leg, complete with stocking and garter, which he held up for the audience to laugh at.

Another bad moment for me was when a young comedian came to our door one night, shaking and sobbing. "You've got to help me," he blubbered. "They're going to kill me."

Stella drew the man in and attempted to soothe him. I hovered in the background, mouthing words like "He can't stay here. Make him go away." All the time I had the feeling that he probably would stay if Stella felt he was in real danger outside. She questioned him for a while, then made a few telephone calls and apparently having assured herself that he would be safe at a hotel, sent him to one.

She explained to me that by showing too much attention to a certain show girl he had incurred the ill-will of a bullying bouncer at one of the night clubs. The situation was not uncommon and you couldn't blame the boy for his panic, since now and then somebody really did get shot up.

People who had been in New York longer than I claimed that Prohibition was to blame for the violence that extended even to little neighborhood shops. If the

owners of these small businesses refused, or could not afford, to pay protection money to gangsters, their establish-
ments were wrecked and proprietors and helpers were
often injured. I saw this happen to a little tailor whom I
had long patronized. The hoodlums gave him a black
eye, then shredded his materials, smashed his equipment
and made rubble of his shop. His customers took up a
collection for him but he went away from there. He said
vehemently that he never wanted to see the neighborhood
again.

My own contributions to the era of nonsense, delightful or idiotic depending upon the point of view of the be-
holder, were rather feeble and pointless. The chief one
after the shimmy lesson was getting my hair cut.

Up to then only a few heroic souls had essayed this first
expression of feminine freedom. When I said that I was
going to get my hair cut, a friend sent me to the Ogilvie
Sisters (seven of them ran a hair salon) and one, Miss
Mabel, the gay, red-haired, next to youngest of the sisters,
did the deed. She first begged me, though, to be sure. I
said I knew what I wanted and, shutting my eyes tight,
told her to go ahead.

Snip, snip went the scissors, for hours it seemed. Then
Miss Mabel said, "Now you can open your eyes." I did—
and after one look at the shorn scarecrow that confronted
me in the mirror, burst into hysterical weeping. My hair
had been curly when I was a little girl and it still waved—
at least it always had waved. Now it hung lank and spirit-
less about my stricken face.

You could hear my sobs all the way down Fifth Avenue.
Poor Mabel tried to comfort me—and all the other Ogil-

vies tried, too. But it was no use. Days passed before I could forget my hair (or lack of it) enough to face my fellow men without shame.

Many of the very modern women I met wore short hair as a badge of courage. They were always steamed up, these champions of equality and workers for women's rights. Also they were good for an outraged statement on any dull day.

"We are *not* free," they would rage at the drop of a question. "We'll never be fit for responsible positions until we get rid of the disabilities under which we now live. . . ."

Mrs. Oliver H. P. Belmont was one of the very social, very rich, very angry women whose agitated activities I often covered. On one occasion, after delivering herself of a denunciation of men for spoiling women, condescending to women and treating women as toys, she came out with a recommendation that women form a union. This made fine headlines but at the end of a week she was on to some other plan for the betterment of our sex. There was plenty of room for improvement, as I found when the president of the Equal Rights Association invited me to make the rounds with her after midnight on a weekday night to demonstrate just how well the state law prohibiting women from working after twelve was operating.

We found that men on the post-midnight shift were not only better paid than the women in the early hours, but they were able to get by with doing much less work than most of the women. My story sarcastically described the sleepy men in their easy jobs, and added that the state government took pains to protect its working women's "all-night scrubbing privileges."

Among other oddities, Stella introduced me to the

strange noises that had been named radio, and dragged me about to little haunts where it was either being performed or heard. This was not so much to increase my general knowledge as to equip me with information for stories that would legitimately include her Leo Feist songs. So quite often my signed articles in the *Mail* mentioned popular ditties.

There was one little yarn about a sparrow with his leg caught on a twig in the one tree on our block (this was when we lived in the West 40's) and ladies leaning out of the windows of a nearby theatrical boardinghouse to worry about the bird and cheer his rescuer on—a little boy who for 50 cents offered to climb up and free the captive. I'm sure that Stella didn't arrange this scene, but I'm not so sure she didn't rush the organ grinder, complete with monkey, to the spot. Certainly she arranged for him to play "Three O'clock in the Morning"—one of her songs—not once but three times, and of course it got into my story.

"My Man," I think, was the opus she was plugging when she took me somewhere down on the river front where we heard a jazz band performing way over in New Jersey. Then there was the time we went to New Jersey in buses accompanied by an array of newspaper people in evening clothes to hear her client, Paul Whiteman, play "Three O'clock in the Morning" for the Prince of Wales. The Prince was fond of substituting now and then for Paul's drummer but he was in London this time and so far as I know never heard our serenade, but Stella got her story anyway.

At the time of my forcible introduction to broadcasting, radio boasted of an audience of two million. To quote me on one occasion, "The studio is a large bare room furnished with a grand piano and an apparatus that looks like an electric heater. The singer or speaker stands before this." The singer on this occasion was Lydia Lipkowska, who along with Frieda Hempel, Percy Grainger and a few other musical long-hairs had dared to pioneer in an effort to reach the unseen audience. Lydia simply stood in front of the apparatus, her accompanist took his seat at the piano, and they produced the aria from Rimsky-Korsakov's *Snow Maiden*.

After the song concluded, Miss Lipkowska ducked out of the way and the announcer grabbed the object that looked like an electric heater to announce her next selection. Then he jumped out of the way to make room for the singer again. This broadcast brought a letter from the frozen North. A man all alone in a little snow hut heard Lipkowska's singing about the snow maiden and wrote of the thrill he'd had.

A while later I went to Sunday morning services at St. Thomas' Episcopal Church and wrote a column about the Rev. Dr. Ernest M. Stire's sermon—heard, the press notice said, not only by the four hundred attending his fashionable church but by two million other worshipers, some gathered around receiving sets set up in barns. Apparently those two million who had sets available were fondly believed to listen constantly.

13. The Women

MY VERY worst moment on a newspaper, I guess, was when a dying woman, swearing me to secrecy, confessed that she'd murdered her husband. What does a real newspaperwoman do with a piece of information like that? Perhaps I proved then that I wasn't a real newspaperwoman for I did nothing. She was dead before morning and though I was so terrified then that I thought I could never forget her, now I can't even remember her name.

Though I wasn't a *good* reporter, I was very proud of being one at all. We women on papers hadn't many illusions about ourselves. With a few exceptions we seldom took time to fuss about our faces or our clothes. Anyway, we couldn't be very stylish on the money we had to spend. Men were always better paid, yet the editors of the twenties knew that women reporters worked harder and were more conscientious.

It's hard to explain the fascination of newspaper work. I am sure that men feel it as much as women and once you've had it, no matter where you go or what you do, no matter how much money you make or even how famous you become, your proudest boast is still that you were once a newspaperman.

It certainly wasn't an easy life. There was no union and you sometimes worked 24 hours without sleep and a dried-out sandwich for food.

People were frequently snooty and downright rude. When you began on a story you were as nervous as a race horse at the starting post, a hard little lump of fear in your stomach. Maybe this time your luck would run out. Maybe you would have to report failure and endure the quizzical looks of the men. In spite of all the people you found who were glad to talk for publication, you always believed that the next person wouldn't and then what should you do? When he did talk and was overeager about it, you were a little chilled for you saw him as a publicity seeker. Besides, you were afraid he'd told the same story over and over to other reporters, plus some fascinating details he hadn't given you. And you worried that the other reporters might handle the story better than you, anyway.

Much, much later, when your copy was turned over to the desk, you had time for a new set of torments: what the copy reader, the headline writer and even the typesetter would do to your precious creation—and where it would land in the paper. You griped if everything wasn't as you'd hoped and you threatened to quit, too, but you didn't mean a word of it.

You might be a coward off your job, but even the puniest would push through fire lines, walk proudly into police cordons on an assignment. You could even make a murderer feel you were his best friend, to get his story.

Naturally we never talked in this sentimental fashion to one another when we met on assignments. Mostly we didn't talk at all for fear of giving something away. We believed in scoops and to get one any of us would lie to his best friends. One at least of my colleagues, all unbeknownst to me, regarded me as an enemy and pilloried me in a novel. I sounded so horrid that I didn't recognize myself until a friend pointed me out. That girl taught me a good lesson—that what we do is much more important to ourselves than it is to anybody else. The reason she hated me, I discovered, was that she thought I had commented disapprovingly about her affair with a married man. The truth was that I knew very little about her or her behavior and seldom gave her a thought, either approving or disapproving.

If I had picked one reporter (besides Zoë) to change places with, I think it would have been Ishbel Ross, named by Stanley Walker, hard-boiled city editor of the New York *Herald Tribune*, as his favorite newspaperwoman. There was something reassuring and solid about Ishbel's clear, honest gaze and her forthright manner. I enjoyed, too, the lilt of Scotland in her speech when she said my name. Also, since she worked for a morning paper and I for an evening one, there was no real rivalry between us. Apparently professional competition wasn't an important item with her anyway, for she married her biggest competitor on many news stories, Bruce Rae of *The New York Times.*

Another of my great favorites was Emma Bugbee, also on the *Herald Tribune.* As Ishbel says in her excellent *Ladies of the Press,* Emma has seen city editors, managing editors and even editors come and go. I learned from her (at least I tried to learn) to wear a noncommittal smile even when everything was going against me. Though there's no question that tears always worked better for *me.*

The women I particularly feared—the dread of being scooped was ever present—were the ones on afternoon papers: Jane Dixon on the *Telegram* with her many years of experience; Marguerite Mooers Marshall on the *Evening World*; Catherine Brody and Marian Spitzer on the *Globe;* Julia McCarthy on the *Journal.*

Jane was one of the first newspaperwomen to cover a prize fight and once I went along to a minor bout and sat beside her. I hid my face every time one of the combatants hit the other, so it seemed rather futile to try to write about the event and I gave up any idea of becoming a sports reporter.

Marguerite Mooers Marshall was my special despair. She seemed to care even less about clothes than the rest of us and usually her hat was perched on the extreme back of her head and in dire danger of becoming unmoored. But she invariably knew the exact question to ask and on a mass interview we all waited for her to fire first. What particularly awed me was the fact that she never took a single note, and yet when her story came out in the *Eve-*

ning World all the statements, even statistics, were those I had painstakingly written down.

I met Julia Harpman, pretty, kind and poised, on the Joseph Elwell murder case, which was never solved. She also met Westbrook Pegler on that story and later married him.

Whist-Expert Elwell was found dead, sitting bolt upright in his chair, a bullet through his forehead. It was a sensational story, complete with rumors of beautiful women, wicked gamblers and law-breaking bootleggers.

Julia had come onto the *News* about the same time I began on the *Mail* and we often saw each other in the elevator. She was not hard-boiled but she had a natural courage and daring that I had to nerve myself to and sometimes never achieved. She would stay on a story until she dropped from fatigue and never feel faint even when she saw (and I still shudder at this) the bones of a murdered baby being separated from the clay in which he had been buried for 10 years. She also fearlessly planted herself next to at least one suspected murderer and eavesdropped upon his conversation. The fact that if she had been detected she might have got a bullet through her head didn't seem to faze her.

Mild-mannered, soft-voiced Grace Robinson, who had edited the *Mail* woman's page, also—much to my amazement—became one of the most illustrious of the town's crime reporters. This, of course, was after she'd left the *Mail* and teamed up with the *News*.

Some of my sister reporters (Louella Parsons, for one) tried to dress me up and put a bit of starch into me. Evidently I seemed to those with real push a rather poor, flimsy thing. Yet one asset I had was determination. I agonized and apologized but I kept stumbling along, even when I had no real idea where I was going.

The shock of my newspaper career was a girl named Imogene Stanley, a blue-eyed, golden-haired creature who was striking-looking enough—including her figure—to be a model. Moreover, she wore charming clothes and seemed a fairy princess in comparison with the rest of us Cinderellas. She was so out of the common run that it was fitting she should be the one to dance with a real prince —the Prince of Wales himself, who was my knight in shining armor from my teens on. On one trip to England I stood in line to shake hands with him at a public affair and I was actually trembling as our eyes met and he said "How dja do." So I didn't blame Imogene a bit when after fox-trotting all evening with the Prince at the Château Frontenac in Quebec—he thought she was a debutante—she refused to write a personal-experience story for her paper, the *News*. Her editor, who had bought her a society girl's wardrobe and even furnished a chaperone to help along the deception, was perhaps justifiably annoyed but she held firm.

After that I looked more wonderingly than ever at Imogene, for surely she inhabited another world than mine. Finally I could resist no longer the pull of the romance on my imagination and tried unsuccessfully to write a fiction story about the girl who danced with the Prince of Wales and refused to cash in on her experience.

I've always been a reluctant joiner, so it startles me to reflect that I helped start the New York Newspaper Womens Club. The club was the idea of Martha Coman, one of a group of women reporters who followed the suffrage movement through to the vote. The reporters had enjoyed drinking tea together from time to time and the club was an effort to continue the pleasant association. My thought was that being with other writers might help me with my great novel. I had never lost this ambition nor the conviction that I would achieve it. The job on the *Mail* was just marking time. Some day my real writing would begin. I never talked about it. I just quite happily took it for granted until one day, sitting in the *Mail* office, I was reading over my story for the day.

Suddenly, as I reached the end, I began to feel dizzy and sick. For a moment I couldn't even see the last line. A voice inside me was saying: "This is all you're capable of. This is the best you can do. You are a third-rate writer and you'll never be anything else."

The worst was that I knew instantly it was all true. I realized that the story before me was written as well as I could write, yet it had nothing of distinction. How long I sat there, I don't know. Maybe minutes, maybe hours. And when I tried at last to stand up, my legs crumpled under me. I guess I screamed. Anyway, people rushed to me. I couldn't speak to tell them what was wrong. Even Mr. Stoddard came. "Telephone for my car," I heard him instruct his secretary. Jack Reardon, the city editor, helped me downstairs. He told me to take a few days off and I drove away in the boss's limousine.

Stella called a doctor. The doctor said I was suffering from nervous exhaustion. He advised an ocean voyage. When he'd gone, Stella and I looked at each other.

"How can I take an ocean voyage?" I asked hopelessly.

"Of course you can take an ocean voyage," Stella, the dauntless, assured me. "There's a day steamer that goes right out into the ocean. We'll take it."

We did, too, next day. By that time I was able to walk. We discovered a hermit living in a swamp. I got a story about him and felt better.

By Monday I was at work as usual. The first pain had worn off. But sometimes I'd think, Reporting won't last forever and I'd ask myself, "What'll I do then?" I felt guiltily that I should break away, that even if I was never to be a great writer, I should try to do magazine articles. Everybody told me they were only longer newspaper feature stories. But my regular stint seemed to take all the energy and imagination I had.

Then one day in the subway going to the office, I read in my morning paper that the *Evening Mail* had been sold to Frank Munsey. We all read about it on the way to work. Nobody had heard a whisper that such a deal was contemplated. I reached the office in a kind of daze and found my fellow workers there, all looking as if they had been bashed on the head. None of us said much, we just sat. A rewrite man who hadn't seen the morning papers arrived in high spirits and after a cheerful greeting stood perplexed looking at our dour faces. It was a relief to tell somebody, and we did, almost in chorus.

He thought at first we were joking.

"But I just got a raise last week," he said as if that would change everything. Then he sat down suddenly on one of the squeaky revolving chairs. He looked like the rest of us now—oddly surprised, anxious. We were all thinking the same thing: How shall I get a job? What will happen to *me?*

The men with families, especially the ones in debt, were trying to decide how to break it to their wives. One or two who had, like me, contracts with a while to run, seemed just as concerned as the rest, and *I* certainly was.

166

Somebody suggested listlessly that maybe we'd all get jobs on the *Telegram* with which, according to the story in the *Times,* the *Mail* was to be combined. But we didn't really believe we would, for just a little while before the *Globe* had been sold to Mr. Munsey to be also merged with the *Telegram* and lots of newspaper people were left without jobs.

About this time the office prankster, bored with the pessimistic atmosphere, alerted two of the brighter, younger spirits and the three set to work constructing a cardboard casket and tombstone for the *Mail* with an effigy of Mr. Munsey to stand beside it.

When the first edition came up, we all grabbed for it and there on the front page were two announcements, one signed by Mr. Stoddard, the other by Mr. Munsey. Tomorrow would be the final issue of the *Mail,* they said. My usual by-line story was on page three. I had covered the annual poultry show the day before: LURE OF CHICKEN RAISING CATCHES MILLIONAIRES AND MECHANICS ALIKE, proclaimed the headline. My last story for the *Mail.* For all I knew, the last time I'd ever have a by-line.

We were all told to report to Mr. Keats Speed at the *Telegram.* Zoë Beckley got a job and a few of the others were taken, too. I wasn't. Even though under the terms of my contract Mr. Munsey would have to pay me $100 a week for nearly a year, they didn't want me. They said they already had too many feature writers.

For once, I didn't cry. After I left the office I walked the streets, distraught and miserable, until it was time for Stella to come home that night. She had heard the news and had been trying to reach me. She was exultant for me.

"This is your great chance!" she assured me. "You'll be

paid $100 a week for months and since you won't have to do a thing for it you can begin to write for magazines. I have an idea right now for your first article—Jazz and Paul Whiteman. The *Saturday Evening Post* will buy it, you just see if it doesn't."

14. The Amber Beads

STELLA KARN was a very determined woman and a born impresario. She had made up her mind that I would write the life of her client, Paul Whiteman. Though I hadn't the slightest notion how to do it, next morning I began. Stella equipped me with a giant pile of copy paper and a dozen well-sharpened pencils. Later that day she added a lot of Whiteman clippings, including one run from all over the country that showed Paul being crowned

King of Jazz by Jeanne Gordon, the singer. This had happened *in absentia,* rather in the manner of a scholar getting a Ph. D. by proxy. Whiteman was on tour at the time and a song plugger friend of Stella's sat in for the photograph. Later Paul's head and body were carefully superimposed under the crown.

Pops, as the big orchestra leader was already affectionately called by his men, was the kind of material that Stella liked to work with. He was intelligent enough to recognize a good publicity idea when he heard it and adventurous enough to go along with it.

Stella's circus background inclined her toward superlatives, so it was natural enough that she should make Whiteman King of Jazz. I found her one day scribbling busily a whole list of circus adjectives, apparently with some notion of further glorifying Paul by dubbing him the Calathumptic (her favorite adjective of all) King of Jazz.

"What *does* calathumptic mean?" I probed, not for the first time.

As usual, this sent Stella into an ecstatic delirium.

"Why, it means the biggest, the best, the most sensational, the greatest . . ."

When Whiteman's orchestra was slated to play in a musical revue, she planned for him a real calathumptic entrance—on an elephant. Then came one of her few frustrations. Whiteman refused.

Stella was as persistent as the tide. He wouldn't ride an elephant. Then how about a horse?

She finally wore Pops down and on the opening night of the engagement, Whiteman, astride a magnificent white charger, rode onstage. The crowd applauded wildly. Stella was smiling and nodding happily out front. Mr. W.

and the steed walked to center stage and then the horse, instead of facing the audience as planned, calmly turned his back to the seats, lifted his tail and—as Whiteman wrathfully and with old-fashioned delicacy later accused—"committed a nuisance."

Not for one minute did this episode change Stella's mind about the charm of this type of entrance. Years later, we had a bitter quarrel because I refused to ride into Madison Square Garden on an elephant for my tenth radio anniversary. And, five years after that, we had another disagreement (mild word!) on the same subject about the Yankee Stadium. When Stella was finally convinced she couldn't get me on an elephant, she calmly proposed landing me on second base in a helicopter. (I walked into both the Garden and the Stadium—two of my infrequent victories over the indomitable Stella.)

It was evident that I was not going to win the battle about jazz, but one morning, as I was tearing up leads and complaining acidly that I didn't know how to write a book, a polite note came from Mr. Keats Speed informing me that a Mrs. Aida de Acosta Breckinridge had asked Mr. Munsey to lend her a good bright newspaper person to help her at the American Child Health Association of which Secretary of Commerce Herbert Hoover was president. Mr. Speed said he had suggested me—obviously not because he considered me a bright newspaperwoman or he'd have had me writing on the *Telegram,* but undoubtedly because under my contract Mr. Munsey had to keep on paying my salary for the better part of a year and Mr. Speed figured they might as well get some good of me. He promised that the loan would take only about a month of my time. Under the circumstances Stella thought I'd better agree.

I did, rather discontentedly, though glad to give up the book.

I didn't dream for a minute that I was going into something that would cause me to feel like a sort of Clara Barton. May the first is to the world a time for hanging May baskets or staging Communist parades, but to me it will always be Child Health Day. I am proud that I had a small part in bringing the first Child Health Day about, and at one time I hoped the idea might revolutionize the lot of children everywhere.

Mrs. Breckinridge was the one who thought up the plan and suggested May 1 as the date, partly because it held the connotation of spring, youth and beginning again, but mostly, I suspect, because it was her daughter Alva's birthday.

I had heard of Aida Breckinridge as one of the beautiful de Acosta sisters. Two of the others well known in New York were Mercedes, actress, and Rita, society woman. Their doings were always material for society and gossip columns and their dark exotic beauty had been recorded by the best portrait painters of the day.

My first interview with Mrs. Breckinridge convinced me that I had ideal material for publicity—a good cause and a well-known person to hang stories on. So I either used her name or dragged her around in person whenever I had to approach a newspaper.

We both got absorbed in the child health campaign and felt that everybody ought to be as concerned as we were. Hence we were able to be both convincing and determined. We pulled it off, too: May 1 that year was celebrated all over the country with speeches, Maypole dancing, parades and resolutions designed to promote child welfare.

I really enjoyed the few weeks and Aida, who was an amazing combination of naïveté and sophistication, apparently had a fairly good opinion of me. In fact, her loyalty got me into trouble. She wrote such an enthusiastic letter to Frank Munsey about me and my work that he, who had probably up to that moment never even heard of me (my dismissal had been handled, of course, by representatives), raised quite a fuss in the office.

"Who is this woman anyway and where is she?" he demanded. "If she's so good, why isn't she working on the *Telegram* right now?"

When Mr. Munsey asked a question like that, everybody snapped to attention and did something quickly. That was why I got, all on the same Friday, a special delivery letter and a telegram ordering me to report to the *Telegram* for work on Monday.

My feelings were still hurt about my dismissal with pay. (They don't want me even though they have to go on paying me one hundred dollars a week until next January, was my constant plaint.) Now after I had taken them at their word, they wanted to change their minds. I didn't think it was fair.

Also I knew from bitter experience that if I went back to a newspaper I would never get the Whiteman book done, for in all the years on the *Mail* I had accomplished simply nothing in the way of writing except my regular daily stint, and while I didn't really want to write a book, I had promised.

I told my troubles to one of my old bosses and he advised me to write a letter of protest to Mr. Munsey. He even suggested what I should say. Sure enough, I got a prompt answer signed by the great man himself asking me to come to see him at the *Sun* office early on a morning that week.

First I was pleased, then frantic. For two nights I didn't sleep because I was going over and over in my mind what I should say and do when I met the ogre of Park Row. The man who was reputed to buy newspapers just to kill them. We all resented him with reason, for his ruthless ways created a lot of unemployment in our profession.

I dreaded that interview more than I had ever dreaded anything in my life, but I made up my mind that whatever happened, whatever he said to me, I *wouldn't* cry. My former boss had cautioned me specifically against that, having had all too much experience with my unfortunate and immature tendency to burst into tears when, as one of my disrespectful housemates put it, "anybody looks at her crossways."

Arrayed in my best on the fateful morning—a blue silk with white collars and cuffs and my Sunday hat—I set forth well ahead of time. One of Mr. Munsey's known prejudices, I had heard, was against tardiness. Another, I knew, was against women, so I determined at least to be a woman on time.

Early as I was, Mr. Munsey was ahead of me and he didn't keep me waiting an instant. As I walked in he looked at me coldly and ordered me to tell my story. He had my letter before him and as I talked kept glancing from me to it. His eyes were blue and glacial. His hair was gray—he was seventy then—and he was tall, spare and straight, a menacing figure.

Uppermost in my mind as I tried to explain my situation was the determination not to cry. So I suppose in my effort to control my shaking voice I sounded aggressive, and to him, insolent. At any rate, he soon halted me with scathing contempt on his face and in his voice.

"Well, miss, if I'd known you were going to be uppish

like this I wouldn't have seen you at all. They told me not to," he declared coldly.

That did it. I fought against crying and the harder I fought the more I cried.

The effect on Mr. Munsey was amazing. I had my head down on his desk by that time so I didn't see him get up, but I felt his hand on my shoulder.

"There, there," he soothed, and even his voice had changed completely. "At first I thought you were one of these hard, modern women. I'm just glad to see that you're not."

He kept patting my shoulder.

"Don't worry about this," he counseled. "I'll have Speed help you find a job. I don't think you'll get $100 a week for it, but that's all right. We'll pay the difference."

Wiping my eyes I explained to him that I was trying to write for magazines. That interested him because he also owned magazines.

"You might show what you do to Mr. Davis [Bob Davis, editor of *Munsey Magazine*]," he suggested kindly, but added: "I doubt if you'll be much good in that line. Magazine writing is hard and quite different from newspaper writing."

Before I left him my tears were all dried and we were talking about how wonderful my mother was. He had evidently been devoted to his own mother, for the subject seemed to strike a sympathetic note. He was interested also to hear that I was born on a farm and that I had been earning my living since I was sixteen.

"I've earned my living since I was seven," he told me. "And I got to New York with $40 in my pocket."

He didn't say it, of course, but I'd heard he was worth at that moment about $40 million.

He saw me to the door, shook hands, wished me luck and we parted the best of friends.

Mr. Speed, who had been present during the interview, followed me into the outer office.

"He means what he says," he assured me, "so don't you worry: your check will reach you every week until the contract is ended."

I was almost afraid to tell my experience to newspaper friends, for they without exception detested Frank Munsey and scoffed angrily at my contention that he could be kind. When he died and left his millions to the Metropolitan Museum, there were some pretty caustic editorials by fellow newspapermen. One said he contributed to the journalism of his day "the talent of a meat packer, the morals of a money-changer and the manners of an undertaker."

I felt really sad at such denunciations, and even though it got me into many an argument, I defended Frank Munsey from then on. There was a delightful little sequel to our meeting. Mrs. Breckinridge got the American Child Health Association to send me $200 as a gift. I promptly mailed the check to Mr. Munsey under what I believed to be our agreement, explaining where it came from. He just as promptly returned it to me, with a note that said presents don't count.

The checks for $100 continued to come every week until the end of the contract, January 1, 1925. And since the story of Paul Whiteman wasn't finished until after that, I never had any earnings to turn in.

I was still nervous about the book-writing project and it was only after a talented and famous writer friend, Rose Wilder Lane, had explained to me that a book is just a series of short pieces that I was able to stumble ahead.

Rose did a great deal more for me than merely *explain* how to write a book, but she forbade me ever to mention the fact to anybody or to give her any public thanks.

"I'll deny it," she warned me, "if you ever say that I helped you."

Somebody suggested afterwards that she believed I would do a bad job and didn't want to be involved. But I know that wasn't the reason. Rose helped a lot of would-be writers out of the goodness of her generous heart and I was lucky to be one of them.

Whiteman wasn't an easy person to get material from. In the first place, he was working hard, preparing to launch a long-time dream to make a lady out of jazz. He felt that jazz was real American music and that it should be honored as such. With this in mind, he was arranging a concert to which he intended to invite the serious music critics in order to convince them of the merits of his medium. He thought of having the affair in Carnegie Hall, but settled that first time for Aeolian Hall. Later he did the program in Carnegie as well as all over the country.

He had a banjo virtuoso in Mike Pingatore, and many men like Ross Gorman, saxophonist, and Ferde Grofe arranger—men who were considered geniuses in their lines.

His singer was a melting Irish tenor, black-haired Morton Downey. And young George Gershwin wrote *Rhapsody in Blue* on order for the concert.

I heard the program first at Aeolian Hall and later from stages all over the country, for having made an honest woman out of jazz, as the feature writers put it, Paul then took her across all state lines.

Stella always said that Whiteman was one of the best musicians of our time and had a real grounding in fundamentals. His father was head of music in the Denver schools and had rigid standards for his son. He was rather startled and saddened when Whiteman broke away from his training in the classics and found work in California playing the violin in a jazz band. However, it looked for a while as if he had no reason to worry, since almost immediately Paul was fired from his first job because the conductor said he couldn't jazz.

One of my chief difficulties in writing the book was to get Whiteman to myself for a few hours. He was a good source of copy when he stopped long enough to talk, though a trifle vague on names and dates. (That's the main trouble, I've found, in writing books with other people. They remember the important things, such as what happened and even what people said, but they get mixed on chronology and now and then actually get one person's name confused with another's, and attribute action to the wrong person.)

My best course, I discovered, was to trail Mr. Whiteman on his travels. When I ran out of material I would hop a train and meet him in Cleveland, Indianapolis, Louisville, or wherever he happened to be giving a concert.

Paul is one of those who never stand if they can sit and never sit if they can lie down. On occasions when I would catch up with him on the day he was to give a concert, he would establish himself in bed, with me and my pad and pencil in a chair by the bedside.

After the free and easy theatrical tradition, it apparently never occurred to him that I might be embarrassed that on these occasions he was always attired in pajama bottoms, a sheet pulled to his chin. The trouble was that when he'd start talking the sheet would slip down and down and I, not knowing at first about the existence of the pajama pants, would get panicky, especially since at the outset he had telephoned down to the hotel desk that he was not to be disturbed for two hours. But he invariably soon wanted ice water, which the bellboy would bring and —perhaps I only imagined—stare curiously at the picture the two of us made.

I especially enjoyed the meals I used to have with Pops. He was a mighty trencherman and I wasn't so bad myself at putting away food. One of our favorite menus was corned beef, cabbage and boiled potatoes with lots of butter for the potatoes and a mixture of mustard and horseradish for the corned beef. We usually finished off with hot apple pie and vanilla ice cream.

I never hear the *Rhapsody in Blue* without a feeling of nostalgia because before I finished the book I got to identify myself with Paul and the band. George Gershwin even then was quite unashamedly confident about his own talent. He had a disarming way of talking about himself that would have sounded like outrageous bragging in anybody less talented.

To my great surprise "Jazz" did sell to the *Saturday Evening Post* just as Stella had predicted and that wasn't all. It was featured on the cover and the first installment led the magazine. Even more important to me was the signature. When I was ready to send it to the *Post* I asked Stella how I ought to sign it.

"Oh," she said carelessly, "why don't you just put 'By Paul Whiteman and Mary Margaret McBride.' They'll fix it any way they want to, anyway."

I did what she suggested, and wonder of wonders, though it was all in the first person, the signature ran just as I had typed it. The money, which was a sizable amount, meant less to me than that first by-line in a maga-

179

zine—and of all magazines, the *Saturday Evening Post*. In the part of the country that I came from, that signature meant that I had arrived.

I cashed the *Post* check (got it all in $100 bills!) and hurried to an Oriental shop called Vantine's on Fifth Avenue. I said to a rather supercilious young man behind the counter, "I'd like to see that string of amber beads in the window, please."

The young man looked me over (I still wore gingham dresses) and, making no move toward the window, said, "They're rather expensive, you know."

"I don't care," I maintained doggedly. "I want to see those beads."

"They cost $200," he warned me, as he started off reluctantly. I said no more, but when he came back with the beads I took them from his hand, reached into my pocket for two $100 bills, shoved them at him and walked out of the shop, leaving him with his mouth open. They were lovely, those beads, like dark luscious honey with tiny insects caught in their depths. I hope the clerk learned that buyers may not always look the part.

15. I Become A Regular Ghost

AFTER the *Saturday Evening Post* bought and ran "Jazz," I naturally kept my contact with Thomas B. Costain, the *Post* editor (now a best-selling novelist) who had seen me through that series. It was his custom to come every Thursday from Philadelphia to New York for the purpose of meeting hopeful authors in one of the prim little parlors of old-fashioned Murray Hill Hotel on Park Avenue.

I was frightened into either total silence or senseless volubility by the editor-in-chief, the great George Horace Lorimer, whenever I'd be summoned to Philadelphia to have lunch with him. But Mr. Costain, with his blue eyes, silver-blond hair and kindly manner, seemed like a real friend to whom I could take ideas without fear that he would think them stupid.

He would listen attentively, mull them over and then say, "That sounds pretty good." Or, alas, sometimes, "I don't believe we could use that." And, to temper the blow, "We had something of the sort not very long ago." Then he would rise, shake hands in courtly fashion, and assure me: "You'll hear from us."

Sure enough, within the week would come an envelope with the *Saturday Evening Post* imprint in the corner, and always he would tell me to go ahead with the ideas he had approved, for if he thought they were good, Mr. Lorimer generally agreed. Mr. Costain's go-ahead was not exactly an order but it was good enough for me.

My next suggestion after "Jazz" was radio (prompted, of course, by Stella Karn, who always seemed able to guess what Mr. Lorimer would be interested in publishing). She also declared that David Sarnoff, important official at RCA and connected with the lively art from its inception, was the person to tell radio's story. Mr. Costain said, "That sounds good." This one, like "Jazz" was to be a first-person story. I would "ghost" it—that is, write it from interviews with David Sarnoff as nearly as possible as he talked.

About all I knew about Mr. Sarnoff was that he had begun a lifelong love affair with radio when, as a teen-age immigrant from Russia, he decided to become a newspaperman. He went down to James Gordon Bennett's *Herald* to ask for a job, but by mistake walked into the office of the Commercial Cable Company. So instead of a copy boy he became a messenger boy, learned Morse code and soon moved on to become an office boy for the Marconi Company of America.

I thought missing a career in journalism by a door was fascinating and became completely absorbed in the adventures of David. He and his pretty wife and their sons had a little house in Mount Vernon. We had some of our interviews there, some at RCA headquarters where strange projects were going forward and where I interviewed inventors, scientists and financiers, most all of whom talked about interesting but obscure subjects. Luckily I could write intelligibly what I could not completely understand and so the articles got done.

Although radio had scarcely arrived then, David Sarnoff was already looking eagerly forward to something he was calling television which meant sending a series of pictures so rapidly through the air that they had the effect of motion pictures.

"The greatest day of all will be reached when not only the human voice but the image of the speaker can be flashed through space in every direction," Mr. Sarnoff said happily. "On that day the whole country will join in every national procession; the backwoodsman will be able to follow the play of expression on the face of every leading artist; mothers will attend child welfare clinics in their own homes; workers will go to night school in the same way; a scientist can demonstrate his latest discoveries to those of his profession even though they be scattered all over the world. . . . I do not think it is fantastic to see

183

in the future great universities broadcasting certain courses, perhaps all courses, and granting degrees on the basis of written examinations."

Mr. Sarnoff has proved to be a pretty good prophet. Two of his dreams, however, are still ahead of us:

"The musical taste of the country is improving," he said. "Even casual surveys which have been conducted to discover, if possible, what radio audiences want, reveal that jazz is losing its place at the head of the list of favorites."

And:

"In the Golden Age of Broadcasting there will be cooperation between stations so that no listener-in will be compelled to miss the big feature on one station while listening to the big feature on another."

Or maybe it's just not yet the Golden Age?

My next ghosting for the *Post* was with a woman.

In the celebrity-ridden city of New York one of the strangest examples of front page build-up I ever saw was Marion Talley of Kansas City, Missouri. I met them all as a *Mail* reporter—Papa and Mama Talley, sister Florence and Marion—when they came on from Kansas City for Marion's first audition at the Metropolitan Opera. Marion was fifteen then, a round-faced, magnolia-skinned little girl with her blond hair in long curls.

Every paper in town turned out to greet the Talleys and the *Mail* assigned me to the story because I too came from Missouri. Sure enough, the Talleys and I got on very well. They took all the fuss calmly as they did everything, though they were surprised that so much should be made of a girl who had merely come to audition at the Metropolitan.

184

After the initial audition and an announcement from the Metropolitan that the girl did indeed have great talent but must get training and the chance for her voice to mature, the Talleys vanished.

I had almost forgotten them, when I ran into them one evening in Central Park. We picked up our acquaintanceship just where we'd left off and sat down on a park bench for a good visit. Marion, her hair still in curls down her back, told me she was studying music and languages and her mother was escorting her back and forth to her lessons. They had a three-room apartment and Papa Talley was back in Kansas City.

In the course of the next four years Marion had another audition and this time turned down an offer from the Metropolitan. She went to Italy for a year of study, came back to New York, sang again for Mr. Gatti-Cazazza, manager of the Metropolitan, and this time signed a contract. She was then nineteen.

Her triumphant debut at the Metropolitan again brought her to the front page. A trainload of Kansas Citians came on for the event, and everybody except the incredible Talleys wept as the young voice rose in the notes of "Caro Nome." Mr. Talley and Florence sat out front perfectly calm amid the excitement. Mrs. Talley was backstage with Marion and when the call came for the singer to make her first entrance, Mrs. Talley wished her daughter luck and sat down with a volume of Tennyson's poems.

When I visited them next morning, already intent on getting a magazine article from them, she explained that she had attended every rehearsal and had heard Marion sing the role of Gilda several hundred times so saw no reason why she should listen again.

Next morning at half past seven when the first of the reporters arrived at the Talley apartment, she found that the family for once had allowed themselves to sleep past seven. They were mortified, they told me, at being caught in such overindulgence. Mrs. Talley combed Marion's hair while the interview went on.

The house was filled with flowers which had been put into all the available vases and crammed into every bottle and glass besides. Some orchids had gotten stuck into a milk bottle and the reporters noted this, greatly to the embarrassment of Mrs. Talley. She was afraid, she confided to me, that everybody would think that the Talleys didn't know what orchids were.

When Marion was twenty-two, *McCall's* magazine (Otis Wiese, the boy-wonder editor, often gave me assignments) asked me to go to see her again, for she had announced that after four seasons at the Metropolitan and about the same number of concert tours she was about to retire to a 900-acre farm in Kansas. I wasn't really surprised because she had said to me after one session at the Metropolitan, "I'm looking forward to buying a nice farm soon where we can have a back yard and chickens."

After her announcement there were rumors that she was going to be married, that she had lost her voice, that she was dissatisfied with her contract, that she was just pretending to retire to get publicity.

Marion told me calmly that it was none of these.

"When I was five years old I used to imagine that somewhere there was a book where everything I was ever to do was written down in advance," she explained. "Now that I'm older I don't see the book so clearly but I am certain that everything I am to do is already settled for me. It is that way about retiring. As you know, I've been thinking about a farm for a long time." So without more ado she retired almost at the beginning of her career.

I felt very close to the Talleys.

Anne Morgan, my next *Post* assignment, was a different kind of story and I was in great awe of her. The handsome, intelligent daughter of an almost legendary Wall Street figure, J. Pierpont Morgan, shunned notoriety and only talked to me for the *Saturday Evening Post* because her friend, Elizabeth Marbury, recommended me and because she wanted her favorite American Woman's Association to be better known.

"It's absolutely extraordinary," she afterwards told anybody who would listen. "The woman never took a note and yet there it was—every word I had said. She must have the most remarkable memory in the world."

I tried for a good while to correct her impression. Then when I realized people preferred her story, I resigned myself to smiling enigmatically. The truth was, sitting in Miss Morgan's elegant little study on Sutton Place with its view of the East River and the barges drifting by, I took extensive notes, but so unobtrusively that she never knew. One of my first lessons in reporting was that it distracts the person being interviewed if he sees the interrogator writing. The knowledge that what he's saying is being put down may even keep him from saying anything interesting or vital. So I taught myself to write with a tiny stubby pencil on a small pad held low in my lap and at the same time to keep my eyes fixed on the face of my interviewee. This was especially important with Miss Morgan because she so disliked interviews. But she was devoted to the American Woman's Association which she had been instrumental in organizing and financing.

Occasionally in the course of an interview Miss Morgan would turn to me and ask me what I thought about life and my sex and I believe she was horrified to find that I had very little real knowledge or appreciation of what had been done for my generation by the women who had gone before. I hadn't known I was taking it all for granted until she scolded me in that deep voice of hers that carried such authority. She always addressed me as "My friend," and sometimes she would invite me to stay for lunch after the interview was over and continue to educate me for what she felt should be my role in the world: telling women and men, too, about understanding women. The belief in some quarters that women were uncooperative especially distressed her.

She hoped the A.W.A. would prove just the opposite and had been persuaded that the magazine pieces might help.

Somehow I got two articles out of her but it was a struggle. She had many taboos. She wouldn't talk about her father or her childhood or what it was like to be a rich man's daughter, or in fact any of her own experiences unless they had to do with the A.W.A.

I'm glad I did the stories, though, for she was my loyal friend through the years, wanting to hear all about what I was doing whenever we sat next to each other at dinners or when, infrequently, she invited me for a weekend at her exquisite country house in Katonah. I remember her affectionately as one of the few people—men or women— I ever knew who wasn't a ham.

Four years after the Hall-Mills case first broke, I, by then a free-lance writer, hung around the courtroom when Mrs. Hall, the stern-faced, self-contained widow of the Rev. Hall, and her two brothers, Henry and Willie

Stevens, were on trial as a result of purportedly new testimony. I saw the sick pig-woman, Jane Gibson, brought from the hospital on a stretcher and dramatically put into a bed that faced the jury. In spite of her condition—she was supposed to be dying—she told with vigor the tale of a trip that she and Jennie, her mule, had made in the dead of night, following what she said she thought might be a wagon containing corn robbers.

She testified that she glimpsed a car in the lane and that the two people in it were Mrs. Hall and Willie. She told of turning her flashlight on them and of hearing shots. Then, she said, she got scared and ran away, losing a moccasin in her flight. When she went back to get the moccasin, she claimed, she saw a big white-haired woman doing something with her hand. She testified quite positively that the woman was Mrs. Hall.

The courtroom was filled that day with trained seals—name writers who were covering for various syndicates and magazines. Billy Sunday and Mary Roberts Rinehart were two of these, and ministers who could knock out a story were in great demand for sermonizing.

For its duration, going to the Hall-Mills trial was as fashionable as going to the races. Society women with enough pull to get seats brought box luncheons; and I've always thought that most of the trained seals, like me, were more curious than interested in the money they got for their stories. Newspaper circulations climbed, and wherever you went the entire conversation was about the trial—people were especially delighted with Willie, who was reputedly slow-witted but who astonished everybody by remaining very calm and sure of himself under pounding cross-examination by the prosecution.

In spite of the pig-woman, the so-called new evidence

didn't change the situation and the trial concluded with the case still unsolved, Mrs. Hall and her brothers free. It was a dreadful ordeal for a brave woman who never showed vengefulness or anything but a calm, rather sad, dignity. My sympathies were all with her, for in my simple belief that sin should be punished I thought the Rev. Hall and his choir leader got what they deserved.

One of my less worthy enterprises as a free-lance was a series of syndicated articles about Peaches and Daddy Browning. Edward W. Browning was a middle-aged New York real estate man who married teen-aged Frances Heenan and, encouraged by the tabloids, carried on a revolting public love-making and equally public quarreling ending in separation. Before I was through, I was sick of myself. I felt dirty and as if I'd sold out to the devil. But everybody kept telling me that a free-lance must take a whack at everything.

Luckily in this free-lance period, after a particularly unappetizing experience I'd usually have a nice one—that often included a trip to Europe.

16. Get Lindbergh's Story

THE name Lindbergh meant nothing in my life. I'm pretty sure I'd never even heard of the man up to that May morning in Paris when Hortense Saunders and I descended to the lobby of our small Left Bank hotel to be greeted by the elevator man, the desk clerk and the headwaiter in the dining room with beaming smiles and *"Félicitations, mesdames, c'est merveilleux, n'est-ce-pas?"*

After the way of friends in New York, Hortense and I

met seldom at home but had run into each other in the rue de Rivoli two days before. I promptly moved to her hotel and we sat up in my room until 3 A.M. playing our favorite card game, which we had named "draw bridge" because we drew for our final hands. Now we looked at each other bewilderedly, even as we smiled and murmured *"Merci"* to the demonstrative Frenchmen.

Why on earth were they congratulating us so fervently? What was marvelous? And what had it to do with us? It wasn't until we saw the great black headlines of the Paris *Herald* that we got some inkling of what had happened in a night during which we had merely played cards and slept. Even then, we didn't feel the full impact until we reached the Morgan Bank where we both had cables in which Lindbergh figured.

GET LINDBERGH'S STORY, frantically commanded Elizabeth Marbury, who always took over from Grace Morse, my usual agent, when there was anything unusual afoot. Hortense's boss sent similar instructions.

A second message for me from Miss Marbury, obviously an afterthought, read, I'VE CABLED AMBASSADOR MYRON HERRICK TO SEE THAT YOU MEET LINDBERGH. GO AT ONCE TO THE EMBASSY.

This Hortense and I did, in a daze, to find the place jammed with reporters from all over the world, an exultant Herrick talking excitedly as he stage-managed everything, and a very weary young man slumped on the stairway leading up from the main hall.

I was told afterwards that the ambassador had a stand-in for Mr. Lindbergh, but it must have been after I saw him that day for there was an air of unmistakable authenticity about that lonely tired figure. I tried to pin the ambassador down to some kind of appointment, but all he would say was, "Later . . ." and then remind me what a wonderful occasion this was.

That afternoon Dorothy Donnelly, author of *Blossom Time,* picked me up in her rented car and took me for a drive in the Bois. As we were coming out of one of the exits to the park the car suddenly stopped and when Dorothy leaned forward to ask for the reason, the driver said in an awe-stricken voice, *"C'est lui—"* Nobody needed to use any name that day in Paris; there was only one *he* for everybody. Sure enough, Lindbergh was having his official French welcome, with the trip up the Champs Élysées to the Arc de Triomphe.

At dinner, an American friend with a little boy in a French school told me that he and the other American children in the school had been carried about on the shoulders of their Gallic schoolmates as a tribute to Lindbergh, their countryman. Everywhere you went, to the little dressmaker, to the milliner, there was only one theme: Lindbergh flying the Atlantic alone. For that day at least he could have been elected President or even King of France.

I never got the interview and Miss Marbury never felt quite the same toward me afterwards. I was no longer her bright girl. But luckily she had already arranged for me to interview her friend Prince Christopher of Greece for a series of *Post* articles.

Prince Christopher, the first royal person I ever knew very well, was never a king, though in his lifetime he turned down three thrones: Poland, Lithuania and Albania. He said he refused to be a king of anywhere because by 1925 sitting on a throne was like sitting on a bomb.

He was a great admirer of Miss Marbury's and often visited her little Sutton Place house where she entertained authors, actors and society people in a discriminating jumble.

She was enormously fat and sat always in an armchair rather like a throne which she filled completely though it was two and a half times the size of an ordinary chair. She served wonderful food but said such funny things that Prince Christopher claimed he often went away from her table hungry because he laughed so much.

Miss Marbury invited me to dinner to meet Prince Christopher. (I already had, at quarantine when he arrived on his first visit with his American wife, but only I knew that.) He wanted to write his life story and since he had little experience in writing, Miss Marbury wished me to undertake the job of ghosting him. I needed very little persuasion, for Prince Christopher seemed an amiable man and certainly he was full of interesting reminiscences. He was kin to most of European royalty, including Queen Victoria who was his great-grandmother, and, as a matter of fact, he was a great uncle of a small boy named Philip Mountbatten, now the Duke of Edinburgh.

The Prince was a man of about medium height, blue-eyed, with brown hair thinning on top. His clothes were always impeccably tailored and in Europe he wore a monocle though in America he often discarded it. When he started to describe his arrival in New York with his wife, the former widow of tin-plate king Leeds, I began to laugh and told him that I had been one of the swarm of reporters who had surrounded him and asked him impertinent questions.

"I like American reporters," he said, "even though I couldn't answer most of your questions, such as what was going to become of Greece and will there be any kings and queens in a hundred years? And the things you made us say that we never thought to say were harmless and sometimes quite clever."

He wasn't so sure about liking photographers, for they made him pose in every imaginable position and kept eying him in disgruntled fashion. Finally one shouted, "Hey, Prince, where's your monocle?" They had heard that he wore a monocle and they expected him to have it on, and white spats too.

At Miss Marbury's that night Christopher told a story about a little American boy who cried when his mother presented him to the Greek prince.

"Where is his crown?" the child sobbed.

I felt just a little the same way. Later, after I'd undertaken the commission of writing his life, I found that he possessed signs of royalty almost as visible as a crown. Though he always claimed he had an inferiority complex, which he thought came partly from being the youngest of eight children, he really had a terrifying self-assurance. Even though he had gone through revolutions, uprisings and the dethroning and even assassination of certain of his relatives, he had kept a poise and an almost arrogant expectation that everything would be done for him. He reminded me of the story about Queen Victoria, who was said never to look behind her to see if a chair was there.

The Prince and I worked for a while in his suite at the Biltmore Hotel in New York and sometimes at my small apartment in the theatrical forties. Hilda Deichler, who became my secretary at that time—and the most loyal and efficient one anybody ever had—claims that Prince Christopher was my favorite subject. Or maybe she thinks I was royalty struck. Anyway, because the Prince wanted to spend the spring at his Roman villa, he suggested that I also go to Italy. Since I had other business in Europe that year, I agreed, and June found me in Rome.

Although he didn't call it that, I think Prince Christopher must have had what Professor Rhine of Duke University calls extra-sensory perception. Unexplainable things were always happening to him.

At his villa in Rome he introduced me to a little dog that he declared often saw ghosts. I never saw the ghost nor was I there when the dog saw it, but Prince Christopher said the animal would bristle, stare at a certain spot and back away. For a few minutes he would bark, show his teeth and snarl, all the time glaring at blank space. After a while he would quiet down.

"Apparently the ghost just goes away," Christopher explained casually.

I'd heard in Rome about the evil eye and I asked Christopher if he believed in it. By that time I was almost ready to believe in it myself. He laughed, and looked thoughtful.

"There are lots of things you can't explain," he mused. "For instance, there was that time at a dull dinner when I pretended I could tell fortunes from cards. I couldn't, of course, but immediately everybody wanted me to try and I began with my neighbor on the right. We put out the cards, but they didn't mean anything to me so I just said to her what came into my head, that she was about to get a letter which would cause her to cross the ocean.

"In a few days I saw her again and she was tremendously excited. Her husband had received a letter calling them both to America. She urged me to tell her something else, so once again we spread out the cards and I, seeing no more than before, predicted: 'You will get another letter which will make it unnecessary for you to take the journey.'

"Would you believe it? In about a week, she turned up with the news that another letter had canceled the trip to America. By this time she believed in me so completely that I began to feel a little ashamed and tried to confess that I knew nothing about telling fortunes—that I had played a rather mean joke on her. She thought I was just trying to get out of telling her anything more and kept at me until I found myself saying words just as I'd done before. 'You will hear of the death of somebody for whom you will put on mourning, but you will not be grief-stricken because the person is not close to you,' I recited."

After that Christopher said he tried to forget the woman, but one day her card was brought to him at a hotel where he was staying. As he descended to the lobby where she waited for him, he caught a glimpse of his visitor swathed from head to foot in crepe mourning veils. His latest prediction had come true and she was after him for more. It was too much. He simply turned and fled. Later he heard that she was in mourning for her mother-in-law, whom she had never seen.

Sitting there on Prince Christopher's terrace overlooking Rome that June day, we had a long discussion about the unexplainable. He contended that it might be possible for certain minds to tune in on other minds and influence them. He felt sure that if you concentrated on something you wanted, you could get it. I thought that over and decided that I agreed. After all, here I was in Rome, Italy, talking to a prince and about as far away metaphorically speaking as you could possibly get from the Missouri prairie farm of my birth, where this kind of talk would have been labeled nonsense.

197

Prince Christopher was always pleasant and even cordial to me—and I'm sure liked me as I liked him—but I never felt close to him as I did to most of my other subjects. This in spite of the fact that he told me many details about himself and others that were too personal to put into our story. The attention of his I remember best was his sending me 12 dozen yellow roses on my birthday. I'd never heard or dreamed of anybody, even a prince, giving anybody 12 dozen roses.

He often asked me to stay to lunch at the villa and the memory of one such luncheon haunted me for years to come. There were three other guests that day, one king and two princes, and we had for dessert the most enormous strawberries I'd ever seen.

Before they came to the table the customary fingerbowl, on a priceless antique lace doily arranged in a plate, was set before each guest. In my excitement at having so many royal table mates, I set the fingerbowl to one side without the accompanying doily and ate my fabulous strawberries off the fabulous wisp of lace. I knew what I'd done before the meal was finished and was scarlet from embarrassment.

A story Prince Christopher told me soon afterwards—now that I come to think of it, maybe he did it on purpose—slightly alleviated my humiliation. He confessed that he still turned red at what he called his unpardonable break at a huge dinner given by Mr. and Mrs. William Randolph Hearst. He and his hostess were discussing American cooking at the very beginning of the meal and she asked if he liked it.

He answered that he considered it excellent. Then he went one fatal step further.

"I can't quite decide about terrapin though. And as far as canvasback duck, it makes me sick."

At that very moment a huge platter was presented to him. On it was the bloodiest possible canvasback duck. To cover his confusion, he took a huge chunk of raw, red fowl at the same time stammering an apology. Mrs. Hearst laughed and he went on trying to eat the duck, though after he swallowed a bite of it he almost literally was sick.

He called Mrs. Hearst a perfect hostess, but I wondered whether perhaps she shouldn't have called the butler and ordered two hard-boiled eggs for her royal guest.

All the time that I was busy interviewing Prince Christopher about the habits and idiosyncrasies of royalty I was leading a very pleasant private life of my own, for I had fallen in love with an Italian named Tony. June is an enchanted time in Rome. Tony was a wonderful guide to the sights, sounds and smells of the city, and it was all perfectly proper for he was introduced to me by a friend. He spoke English with a charming accent but I longed to talk to him in Italian and started taking lessons from an Englishwoman at my hotel. I found Italian easier to learn than French, but then I'd never fallen in love with a Frenchman.

Tony was a Neapolitan—dark-haired, dark-eyed and ardent—and a career man in the government. We never discussed politics but I definitely felt that he feared and disliked the dictatorship. Mussolini was well-entrenched by that time and there was no need for black shirt parades or other public demonstrations of power. But Americans in the city told me that fear and distrust were everywhere.

"Haven't you noticed the typical Roman gesture?" asked a woman who had lived there for some years. "It's a quick look over the shoulder before saying anything that has bearing on government or even personal affairs. They are all afraid that something will be overheard and held against them when a day of reckoning comes."

Tony took me on wonderful excursions in the city and outside. There was one place where we sat often on a hillside, looking down at Rome just as the lights were coming on and eating ham and fresh figs. We went to *trattorias*—country inns, each of which served a distinctive pasta: canneloni, fettucine, ravioli, lasagna, manecotti, spaghetti alla carbonara. One had a version of bouillabaise with mussels and octopus which I never quite got used to; another specialized in roast baby lamb with a faint whisper of garlic. And an artist friend of Tony's always sautéed zucchini blossoms for lunch when I went there.

I thought I would like to marry Tony but I didn't want to live in fascist Italy. Just about this time, too, I decided that I wanted a daughter. Tony never knew that I seriously debated marrying him—he asked me several times —getting pregnant and then hurrying back to the United States where I could have my baby in the land of the free.

I guess I was not really in love but carried away by Tony's way of making me feel like an 18th-century heroine or perhaps it was his taste in restaurants that did so well with varied pasta, amazing wild mushrooms, fragrant wild strawberries. Or it could have been his knowledge of romantic features such as the keyhole in the garden wall of the Villa of the Knights of Malta through which you could see St. Peter's Dome. Anyway, when I finished getting my material on Prince Christopher I was quite ready to leave Italy.

And by the time I reached Paris I had already put the memory away in honeysuckle. Helen Josephy, my old colleague of *Mail* days who was working on the Paris *Herald,* said, "You know what I think, Mary Marg? You have life licked at last. Everything's just the way you want it. I'll bet you never again go through all those awful downs."

I felt rather the same and very superior, too, as you do when you believe you at last have things as you like them. Only by this time I was experienced enough to know better in my heart. But for the next few weeks life was very sweet.

For a long time I had planned a trip to Ireland. I had fallen for one of the oldest stories that ever enlivens the dreams of Irish- and Scottish-descended Americans: that somewhere in one country or the other is a castle, a great family heirloom waiting to be claimed.

My great-grandfather Moore was the one who told me about our castle in Ireland and when I was little I believed implicitly that if only I could cross the ocean, the castle would be waiting for me, complete with moat and drawbridge. I suppose it isn't necessary to say that I never found it, but even before I went there I had something better: a friend I'd met through Miss Marbury who was *born* in a castle. Moreover, her brother still lived in it. Not that I knew all this at the time. Moira O'Brien Bathurst just said casually that her brother was at Dromoland, the family home in County Clare. How was I to guess that the family home would turn out to be a gray-ivied traditional castle set back in a great private park?

I met Lady Bathurst according to plan in Limerick and

we arrived at Dromoland about four in the afternoon. Immediately tea was served by a butler with sideburns beneath an ancient lime tree in a beautiful old garden. The sundial looked as if it had always been in the garden and the peacocks that strutted about in the sunshine also seemed a permanent part of the picture. Fountains were tinkling, roses and stock perfumed the air, and the crumpets and real Irish tea tasted just as I thought they should. Nearby was a lake upon which Moira said she and her thirteen brothers and sisters had rowed when they were little. Once she and two of her younger brothers dropped their oars.

"We'd have drowned, too," Moira reported mysteriously, "if THEY hadn't helped us. Not one of us could swim."

That was the first time I heard such a reference but all the Irish I met afterwards, whether in castles or in thatched huts, talked familiarly and frequently of leprechauns, fairies and others of the wee people, and invariably referred to them as "they." The reason for this seemed to be that the wee people resent being gossiped about and the more cautious you are, the less likely they are to get a grudge against you.

There's a tale in County Clare about one reckless old beldame who did boast of her intimacy with the wee people, and was found one day on the edge of the cemetery, half dead with fright, her body black and blue from the pinching of tiny fingers. She would never talk about the experience but stopped bragging.

Moira took me all over County Clare, into every tiny cottage and to all the little shops that she remembered. She had talked a good deal about a certain kind of jam tart that she and her brothers and sisters used to save up their pennies to buy, and sure enough there it still was and the shopkeeper, too, grown gray, making a great fuss over Miss Moira.

Johnny Murphy, who claimed to be over one hundred, a small fellow who looked a little like a leprechaun himself, became my friendly guide and storyteller-in-chief. When we went by his cottage in the morning, he popped out dressed in decent Sunday black, with an elfin peaked hat perched at a rakish angle, and burst at once into a fearsome tale about some curse that THEY, when offended, had put upon a family so that every member eventually died off.

In one especially horrendous story, the last survivor drowned in no more than a cup of water.

When I went out to the wild cliff of Moher, Johnny urged me to listen hard to try to catch the distant crowing of cocks from Kilstuiffeen, buried by a curse. But although I strained my ears, I could hear nothing except the screeching of the gulls on the cliffs as they dived into the foam, and never a whisper from Kilstuiffeen.

According to Johnny, the bay of Liscannor will dry up when a six-fingered, six-toed wife of a tailor finds a big key on Lahinch shore. This key will unlock Kilstuiffeen and everything will be just as it was when the humans and their houses fell into the sea and the waters closed over them.

"You're heartily welcome," was the invariable greeting of the friendly people in the thatched whitewashed cottages. Then immediately they would put the kettle on so that we could have a sup of tea with a bit of bread and jam. The whole time in Ireland was like an enchanted dream. I'd left no forwarding address with my London bank, and so no news, good or bad, came to disturb the bliss of the blue and gold days. But when I was homeward bound, I began to worry about my mother and long to hear from her. Only a dream world could have put her even temporarily out of my mind.

17. Papa's Boom and Bust

THROUGHOUT the years that I was doing well at free-lancing I went home once a year and once a year my mother came on to New York. In spite of Mama's wonderful disposition, it wasn't always sweetness and light when she was visiting, for Stella and I often quarreled violently—sometimes over how to entertain her. I felt that I ought to know what my own mother would like and

Stella was just as sure that Lizzie, as she called my mother, would prefer her way.

Once when she came to spend Christmas we got into such a hassle over whether she would have her presents in a mammoth stocking Stella had bought for her or the pillowcase I advocated, that my poor mother—who always pretended to be surprised because we liked it that way—couldn't ignore the noise any longer and came to the door imploring, "Girls, let's just not have any Christmas."

We never succeeded in keeping anything from her. One time she came just after we had reoccupied an apartment we had sublet during a summer I had spent in Europe on a story. The subletters had somehow managed to acquire bedbugs and I, knowing how my good-housekeeper mother felt about the small creatures, was determined to keep her from learning about ours.

We'd had the place thoroughly sprayed and fumigated, but once in a while one of the little pests would crawl out of the woodwork. I had done my best and had to leave it to fate that none would appear while my mother was watching. But hardly had she changed into a crisp white cotton house dress after her arrival than she called to Stella and pointed to her spotless sleeve where one of the bugs was crawling.

"Stella," she said quietly, "I think that you and Mary Margaret had better know that there are bedbugs in this apartment."

And with a look of extreme distaste, she squashed the bug, adding with unaccustomed vehemence, "I have never had the filthy things in my house."

Part of my childhood ambition had been achieved: getting to New York and working on a newspaper. Now came the third part. I had saved enough money to take my mother to Europe. This was right after my father had moved the whole family to Florida to live.

Mother got to New York from Orlando in time to buy a few new dresses, be photographed, sign for her passport and help me pack. Then we were on the S.S. *Paris*. Alas, she was seasick—sicker after we gave her champagne which somebody said would cure her. She felt queazy all the way across and was terribly depressed by the time we landed at Le Havre. The strange language and the sense of being so far away from her husband and boys was hard for her. That was when Stella got the bright idea of what she called "deceiving Lizzie for her own good." She persuaded my mother to take a small glass of cherry brandy, disguised as cherry bounce.

Mama knew cherry bounce as a harmless nonalcoholic drink made by certain countrywomen of her acquaintance. She consented to sip cautiously at the sweet liqueur and did become considerably less unhappy. She confided that she had never thought she'd care for cherry bounce but we were left with the impression that she might try a brew of it sometime back home if any cherries came her way.

By the time we reached Paris, she was in fine spirits and from then on seemed to enjoy everything, particularly the flowers in homes and public gardens. At Versailles, she wandered off to look at shrubbery and begonias when we expected her to thrill to the historic Hall of Mirrors. She enjoyed the Petit Trianon where Marie Antoinette had played at being a milkmaid, even laughed out loud at the queen's miniature dairy. It tickled her that a queen should churn butter for amusement.

I bought her a Paris hat that tilted fashionably over one eye. Her arthritis kept her from walking too far in a day but we took it slowly and she spent about as much time as the average tourist inspecting museums and monuments. It was a very sentimental journey for me because I had planned it so long and with such anticipation. Whether it ever meant to her what it did to me I never found out. Certainly her good Scottish common sense pulled me up several times when I was inclined to get too saccharine.

She hurt her foot and had to stay in bed for two days in Switzerland, at one of those brisk, tidy hotels the Swiss do so well. One morning, looking down at her eating breakfast in bed, I thought back to the hard winters in Missouri when she had taken care of my brothers and me if we had the least thing wrong with us, though often she was sicker than we.

"You can be sick as long as you like," I assured her, misty-eyed. But she wasn't in the mood for that kind of nonsense.

"Thank you, Sister, but I didn't come all the way to Europe to lie around in bed," she said tartly.

I had a special assignment that year to write a story about ex-royalty. We went to Doorn, Germany, where we found the ex-kaiser chopping wood and riding on the public bus. We discovered ex-King Manuel of Portugal at Twickenham-on-the-Thames raising ducks and geese for a hobby. Mother got on very well with him for she, too, knew all about poultry. She advised Manuel not to try turkeys. "They are always getting lost," she warned, "and they hide their eggs so that you can never find them."

In the Basque country of Spain near the French border in a little town called Lequatio that smelled of olive oil frying we saw the ex-empress of Austria, Zita, with her angelic-looking brood of blue-eyed, fair-haired children.

We even went to a circus in the town bull ring with the royal family.

The empress was very devout and one morning at 5 o'clock I found her kneeling at prayer in the little church beside a score of fishermen who were asking God a blessing on their catch.

The worst crisis of the whole trip was when we landed in New York and the customs men checked Mama's luggage. We had been keeping something from her for several days. It was a big black headline I had read clear across a dining room in a German hotel. It said: FLORIDA DESTROYED BY HURRICANE.

I dashed out that day and sent a cable to my father, asking for news of him and the boys to be sent to Le Havre, from where we were sailing. The cable never came and all Europe believed Florida was seriously damaged, so I got on the ship not knowing whether my father and brothers were alive. I shuddered every time my mother even mentioned their names and never left her alone with others on the ship for fear that something would be said. Of course nobody knew any more than we did about the situation.

All went reasonably well until the customs man looked at the tag on her baggage. "Orlando, Florida!" he exclaimed. "That's one of the places that was hit by that bad—"

He got no further, for I broke in nervously with some chatter about the things we had to declare. My mother didn't ask him any questions but from the corner of my eye I could see her lips tighten and I knew I was in for it.

As soon as possible she dragged me to one side. "Sister, what did that man mean?" she demanded. "You might as well tell me. I know you are keeping something from me, and I won't have it."

My gentle mother was really angry and I knew better than to try to put her off, so I told her the whole story and promised we would call my father as soon as we could get outside to the public telephones. She didn't burst into tears but she said quite grimly, "If anything has happened to your father and the boys, I'll never forgive myself."

I tried feebly to argue that her being in Europe had nothing to do with the hurricane, but there was no comforting her until we got my father on the telephone and she was sure everything was all right. He was very casual about it. He said, "We've seen worse storms in Missouri."

In a way, the incident spoiled the trip for me because my mother, even when she boarded the train for Florida, was still resentful at my not having told her. She kept saying, "What do you girls think I am? I don't want things kept from me." And it was useless to assure her that we only meant to spare her.

I sometimes think that of the whole trip she enjoyed most the small presents she had bought for the family and the gadgets and souvenirs Stella had loaded her with —a metal replica of the Eiffel Tower, restaurant menus, fans with advertisements for various places, a pressed gardenia from the corsage somebody had sent her, pins with names of places on them (one from Switzerland had a pressed alpine flower inside), pictures of historic spots. After she died I found them all carefully put away by themselves in a sandalwood box. I hope my father and the boys were a good audience for her when she talked of the trip.

One of the exhibits that certainly should have inter-

ested the boys—my father, too—was a program from the
Folies Bergéres, to which we took her after considerable
debate. Luckily the jokes were in French, which she
couldn't understand, but when Josephine Baker came on
stage dressed mostly in a string of bananas round her
waist, I stole a glance at my mother and found her quietly
looking down at her lap. I thought there was a slight flush
on her cheeks, but she made no comment and neither did
I. But I'll bet she told my father about it.

Florida in the mid-twenties was full of men like my
father who, though they had never been conventional
speculators, had really followed that kind of life from the
time they began to work, for certainly nothing is more
speculative than farming. If you don't have a drought,
you have too much rain and everything rots in the ground.
If it isn't too cold, it's too hot. If grasshoppers don't come
to plague you, caterpillars will.

My father was a farmer all his life until he gave that
up to fatten stock—cattle and pigs—to ship to the markets
in St. Louis and Chicago. Between the time the animals
started on their way and the hour of their arrival, prices
could and often did take a nose dive, so that he ended up
in the hole. Even if, for once, good prices held there was
constant danger of animals sickening and dying in droves.

In spite of my frequent fury at my father, which burst
out through the years with considerable regularity, I had
got from my mother a feeling that he was a person to be
sorry for. Yet she fell in love with him because in spite
of his small stature he was a very dashing figure in his
youth.

The first time my mother saw him he was walking

along a high wall at the fair grounds in Paris, Missouri, while the young blades of the countryside looked on, some yelling encouragement, others derision.

My mother held her breath and she always said that from that moment on she had a special feeling for him though at the time they hadn't even been introduced. My father was a ladies' man who kept several girls on the string whereas my mother had one steady solid-citizen type of beau whose chances were practically nil after that day at the fair grounds. My mother always added proudly when she told my brothers and me the story that my father triumphantly concluded his feat of walking the wall by turning a backward somersault, and even the scoffers cheered.

The reason my mother's heart was especially soft where my father was concerned was that his mother had died when he was born and Mama thought that his step-mother hadn't loved him. That was the worst thing that could happen to a child in my mother's opinion—not to be loved. Besides, though his father was a teacher and a scholar, young Thomas Walker was permitted to stop school when he got tired of it. And that was all too soon. After she married him, Mama tried to make up to him through the years for what he had missed as a child. Anything he said was law in our household.

Though we grew to like all his favorite foods, she cooked them primarily not for us but for him. By his plate always stood a pitcher of syrup and another of ketchup. He never ate a meal, company or otherwise, without lavish use of both of these. My mother lovingly shaved his neck each week and cut his hair herself. After they were both long dead I found among my books one that she had been reading on a visit to me and in it the beginning of a letter to him. "My own darling boy," it said in her fine round writing, which remained, in spite of fingers stiffened with arthritis, meticulous and clear all her life.

My father would trade anything—a horse, a mule, a cow, a buggy, a farm. I cannot remember that he was ever discouraged by any of his ventures, though there were certainly those among our friends and relatives who thought that he often showed a lack of judgment and at times got much the worst of it.

Anyway, with his impulsive Irish temperament it was inevitable that once in Florida he should have embarked with zest upon the boom.

He had long dreamed of living in Florida because he had come upon some of those prospectuses that described the state as a place where you could sit and watch in the twilight the fronds of the graceful palms latticed against the fading gold of the sun-kissed sky. And best of all, the one that said, "Work is not work in the Florida sun and lucky Floridians pick golden fruit off their own trees and enjoy it in the leisure unknown elsewhere in the world."

Middle-Western farmers work hard and this sounded like Utopia to my father. Apparently an orange grove didn't need the kind of drudgery that you had to put into a wheat field or an apple orchard. A legacy of a few thousand dollars from a rich aunt made it possible for him to settle up small debts that had plagued him all his life, and then he gathered his family together and set out in his Model T for Florida.

Somebody had told him about Orlando in Orange County and that was where he settled in a flimsy little house surrounded by sleeping porches. Adjoining was an orange grove in fair condition which still, contrary to what my father believed, would require considerable work to make profitable.

You have to learn about orange growing and my father never did. That wasn't what he had come to Florida to do. Much more attractive were the tales he began to hear of the astonishing amounts of money to be made in real estate. Everywhere were optimistic signs promising great profits for infinitesimal investments, and neighbors told him that sometimes you could double and even quadruple your cash by turning over lots without even making your own first payment. Most of the money, of course, was being made along the coast and Orlando, unfortunately, was inland. Even so, the whole state was feeling the effects of the activity around Miami and Palm Beach.

The entire country was in the middle of an era of prosperity. Nobody except a few unpopular prophets of doom even hinted the good times could ever end. So, my father took all the money he had and began to put it down $50 and $100 at a time on lots which he never expected to have to pay for in full. Long before any such necessity as that arose, he firmly believed, he would have turned his investments over for big profits. Of course this was a small-time operation compared to the hundreds of thousands that were changing hands in places that had beaches. All my father expected was that if he put down $50 on a lot, the next fellow who came along would pay him $100 or even $150 for the option.

This was easier and far more stimulating than raising oranges. Papa constantly made calculations on small slips of paper—my mother showed me some of them long afterward. These pathetic jottings indicated that he dreamed he might eventually be worth as much as $100,000, which was just about as far as his great expectations could possibly go.

He was not one to confide in any member of his family, so my mother and brothers had no idea about his operations, some of which of course went on while Mama was in Europe. Soon after she came back he began to seem moody and worried. He would sit on the front porch for hours without talking to anybody. At night my mother noticed that he slept restlessly and moaned and muttered. She was anxious but knew better than to ask questions when he was like that.

Eventually he simply took to his bed and stayed there, a quiet, beaten figure.

It was then that my mother secretly sent for me.

"He's either very sick or he has something terrible on his mind," she told me. She was frantic about him but managed to keep her head so that if he needed her, she'd be ready.

I didn't relish the task but I finally asked my father outright what was the matter with him. I think he was relieved to share the burden, for he made no protest but told me at once. He had to do a good deal of explaining because until that minute I didn't even know there had been a boom in Florida, nor that I was seeing the end of it. The truth was that my father had gotten in much too late. Even when he was paying down $50 and $100 to frenzied salesmen, the land on which he was taking option was already practically valueless.

I remember I lay awake that night on the sleeping porch, with the full moon shining on my face and the honey-sweet fragrance of orange blossoms in my nostrils, wondering what on earth to do. Though I wasn't a very good businesswoman, I felt sure that to put any more money into my father's disastrous venture would be idiotic folly. What was there left then, except to turn the land back to anybody who would take it? Since Papa, like all the other speculators, had paid no attention to investigating titles, recording deeds or other tiresome formalities, there was absolutely no hope of recovering any of his deposits. I found too that his orange grove was heavily mortgaged. I didn't get much sleep that night but by next morning I had formed a plan of action.

I decided that not only would we abandon my father's claims, we would also get rid of the orange grove and the little shack of a dwelling and I would buy my parents a small house. It was rather sad to see my usually domineering father for once quite meek and though I felt he deserved it, I was sorry for him. It seemed strange that no prophetic instinct warned me that I was about to duplicate in my own way my father's folly. Like millions of other Americans, I too had become a speculator. I was playing the stock market on margin. My paper profits—not my earnings, although at that time I was doing very well with free-lance writing—were what made it possible for me to get my family out of their difficulties.

After we found the house I wanted on a pretty little lake in Winter Park which is separated from Orlando only by an arch, I cashed in some of my profits to make the required down payment. I would gladly have cleared off the two mortgages also with paper profits and had the place free and clear, but Mr. H., my rich advisor, was against it. He said, "Oh, no, the money is worth much more invested in the market than in a house." And he added, "Smart business people always have mortgages."

I didn't agree with him then and I certainly don't agree with him now. If I'd paid completely for the house as I had the money at that time to do, I would have been spared many agonizing hours later.

Though I couldn't see any sense to his advice, I thought, What do I know about it? Mr. H. is a millionaire!

One thing I did pay for in full was the landscaping of the small lot on which the house stood. I hadn't had time to learn how fast Florida vegetation grows nor how lush it soon becomes, so I ordered some of everything I saw. I had hibiscus, azaleas, camellias, bougainvillea, lantana, bird of paradise, yucca, several kinds of jasmine, a cherry hedge and down by the lake, bamboo, rushes, palms of many varieties, and at the edge of the water, lilies. I don't entirely blame the nurseryman, for he did attempt to warn me a few times that I might be buying too many plants for the amount of land. But I impatiently brushed him off and went right on picking out everything in sight.

My mother was such a flower lover that I told myself she would have fun with all these exotic plants. I didn't realize that I was hanging an albatross around her neck. It would have taken two experienced full-time gardeners to keep that little lot in condition after I got through. Luckily Florida was now a buyer's paradise. I paid for the house a fourth of what it had cost in boom times and I probably could have got it for less if I had been a better bargainer. Everybody was desperate to sell and very few wanted to buy.

The state at this time looked like a series of ghost towns and villages. The come-ons of the shrewd real estate operators and the shattered dreams of victims of Florida fever were visible on all sides. Driving down a road in the middle of nowhere you would come upon a pair of rusting grillwork gates, opening onto nothing. Sometimes a developer had gotten as far as laying out streets, the only sign of which were posts and markers bearing street names, but overgrown with tall grass and palmetto. The countryside was even more ghostly as you approached the seacoasts. Many speculators, working with marshy land, had planned developments along the lines of Venice and had even dug canals and started to construct stucco bridges. Some of these had been reduced to rubble by the very hurricane which we had concealed from my mother.

So many people had been stripped clean by the collapse of the boom, that the state seemed full of families living in little huts and existing on lean rations. But the prospectuses were right in one thing: life here was insidiously lazy. The sun was warm and comforting and while you couldn't live on oranges and grapefruit, they were yours for the taking; as many as you needed for your individual supply of Vitamin C were supplemented by other tropical products such as avocados and some of the usual vegetables of which there often were several crops in a season.

My mother was homesick for her own sweet peas, pansies, nasturtiums and especially roses, none of which she could grow in the Florida soil. The profusion of other delights never quite made up for the lack of these old friends. She consoled herself finally by accumulating pots and pots of African violets, started from plants brought from Missouri. She had them in every variety: white, pink, blue and purple, double and single. So did her neighbors, for she was constantly giving them not only pots of African violets but her own special kind of fruit and nut cookies, penuche and salt-rising bread.

Though my father could still rise to heights of the old childlike enthusiasm, the Florida catastrophe had a sobering effect on him. Perhaps it also made him less confident that whatever he decided was right. In the old days it seemingly never occurred to him that he could be wrong. Also, with his old-fashioned ideas about woman's place being in the home, it was galling to have me a witness to his humiliating failure. Apparently, too, he began to realize that he was no longer a young man. Sometimes he would say a little sadly at the close of a day, "I guess I'm getting old." This my mother would fiercely dispute. She didn't mind age for herself but my father was still her little boy. I discovered her furious one day at two men who had been pruning the orange trees. She had overheard them calling my father "the old man."

18. My Boom and Bust

MANY attempts have been made to explain why men and women gambled away their entire savings in real estate ventures in Florida and other states that had similar if lesser booms, but by far the greatest amount of print has been given over to surmise about what animated those who in the twenties put everything they had into Wall Street stocks on dangerous margins.

I can certainly answer the latter question about one

person: myself. The only time I put my hard-earned savings into Wall Street was when I thought my paper profits were being swept away and I was told that more margin would save them. I don't know whether Stella's and my experience was unusual or not. At least it was painless up to a point. This man we knew who was fond of us and had a great deal of money simply established credit for us at his broker's. His enormous balance guaranteed us until we had done what almost everybody was able to do in those days—made so much profit that we no longer needed guaranteeing. That is, our first tiny purchases on credit rose in value until we had what was to us in those times a small fortune in paper profits. Then the stocks were sold and we started over again with stocks paid for with the profits.

Nobody seemed able to lose—at least nobody who had the kind of "expert" advice we were getting. I remember coming back from an assignment in Europe in the early fall of 1927 and being shown a check for $21,000 made out to me from the broker. I was just allowed to look at it, and then Stella and our advisor whisked it away and back into the market. They just thought it would be fun for me to see in concrete form my winnings up to that moment. Within a year the amount was quadrupled in spite of my having taken some of it out for a down payment on my mother's house and for other expenditures. Then one day Stella telephoned me in great excitement.

"How would you like to live on Park Avenue?" she asked. I thought she was joking, for I regarded Park Avenue as a very expensive street indeed and far out of the reach of such as me. To my astonishment I soon realized that she was in dead earnest.

"I'm going to buy, and I want you to buy, some rubber

stock," she said. Then she went into a long explanation about how she had been sitting next to some Wall Street man at dinner a while back and he had said that if the lighter-than-air Graf Zeppelin successfully crossed the ocean, rubber stocks would soar. The Graf Zeppelin was about to start the crossing and she thought the risk looked good.

We bought the stock, the Graf Zeppelin got across whatever ocean it had been attempting and we each made enough out of the deal to pay our rent on Park Avenue for two years. At least it *would* have paid our rent for two years if we had then and there taken it out of the market, labeled it "rent" and socked it in the bank. Of course we did nothing of the kind. Nobody was prudent in those times. You sold the stock when it rocketed up and bought another stock, then you sold that after it had risen twenty or thirty points, and used the profits to buy more and more stocks—all on margin until you had a structure like a very tottery skyscraper.

Not that it seemed tottery to anybody else involved in the deals. Stella especially had a wonderful time through all this, for she was sure she knew what she was doing and she was a born gambler. I was not. The transactions couldn't have interested me less. I had been brought up to believe that you worked hard for what you got and the only money I had the slightest confidence in was sweat-of-the-brow earnings. I just went along for the ride in Wall Street.

My whole philosophy about money probably was revealed in those first years in New York when, to keep them safe, I carried around whatever bills I possessed folded up in the band of my hat. The only good the paper profits were to me—except for the little bit that I spent for my family—was to give me a background of confidence in my free-lancing. Even though the money seemed unreal to me, I knew in a vague sort of way that I could call upon it if I had to and so I was kept from that desperate feeling it is so easy to get when you are a free-lance—that is, not on a salary. I suppose not only writers but artists, salesmen and others on commission have the same fears at times.

As a matter of fact, the whole stock market idea seemed sinful to me and I often felt that if I'd had real character, I'd never have gone into it in the first place. I would have been very much an exception if I hadn't been in it, though. I remember once waiting patiently in line at the cashier's desk at Schrafft's, check in hand, while the cashier and the customer in front of me discussed the latest stock the cashier had bought.

Everybody talked stocks—at mealtime, in offices, even in elevators. Now and then a warning voice was raised and once in a while the papers even printed a quotation from some bonehead with a bearish attitude, but who could take any stock in pessimism when U.S. Steel, A.T. & T., New York Central, all the coppers (I remember I had Anaconda and Kennecott) continued to soar? For that matter, it hardly seemed important what you bought. You couldn't fail to make a profit.

In the summer of 1929 Stella and I were planning a trip to Scandinavia with some friends. Just before we left, I had dinner with a man who believed the stock market was going to go down. He boasted that he had never bought a share of stock on margin and he was unhappy about my investments. My whole attitude had become so much a part of the trend that I actually thought to myself, This man is a fool. Though I still didn't believe in the market, I felt superior. I guess it was the old story of pride goeth before a fall.

This was a period of wonderful send-offs for people sailing for Europe. Our ship was beautiful, furnished in light woods and shiny metal and contained every luxury one could dream of. A great party came to see us sail and boxes of candy, nuts and cakes were piled nearly to the ceiling. Quantities of flowers, including corsages for every day on the boat, and baskets of fruit so big the stewards could hardly carry them through the door kept arriving. Nobody could possibly eat all that stuff and I think even the stewards and stewardesses were a little bit blasé about the remains that were turned over to them.

In Copenhagen, Denmark, I visited the great Danish silver shops with my friend Florence Rogatz, who had recently been married to Al Herman. She was buying flat silver for her new home, expensive stuff but simple and beautiful, just the kind I liked.

"Why must people be married to have beautiful silver?" I suddenly demanded of nobody in particular. "I'm going to buy some too."

And I did, not only flat silver but an enormous silver tea set. There was certainly too much of it to carry around the fjords and besides I still had London and Paris on my itinerary, so I said grandly to the clerk, "Just send this to America for me."

Everybody began to explain that it would have to be put in bond and would cost a great deal more than if I took it with me. I imperiously waved away warnings. After all, I didn't have to worry: by the time I got back to New York my paper profits would probably have doubled again—maybe tripled. When you are traveling fast in Europe you don't get much chance to read the newspapers, and anyway, they are mostly in a language you don't understand, so I really had no inkling of what was happening on Wall Street.

True, Stella got occasional reports from her broker but if they caused her any uneasiness she didn't mention it. Even if I'd been at home, I still wouldn't have been forewarned. For in the summer of 1929 stock prices had gone way above anything ever known before. It seemed that there were no limits. The total of brokers' loans climbed to six billions. Businessmen had marveled in 1927 when it had been a mere three and one-half billions. You heard some talk of inflation but you heard a lot more about prosperity.

People said things like, "We've just started!" "Never sell America short!" "I'm going to hold that stock for 500!"

We were in Paris early in September when the market soared to its greatest height. We read about it in the Paris *Herald* and congratulated ourselves. But it didn't occur to us that this was the top. All through September the papers carried stories that if we'd but known it, were signals of disaster. The market would have fits of receding and next day recovering. The financial reporters called it a "nervous market." That is, they did until the week of October 21st. And that was when we got back to New York City.

Our advisor was expecting a recovery that did not come. However, he stood firm. There was a great deal of selling; millions of shares were changing hands every day, so many that the ticker tape could not keep up. Our advisor said the market was just stabilizing itself; that a leveling off was overdue, but that after the shakeout everything would go even higher.

Then came the deluge. On Thursday, October 24, Stella and I had scheduled a big party for Inez Haynes Irwin, who had a new book coming out. We had made arrangements with Dean's, a good and costly firm, to cater for the party. I had ordered a lot of delightful little hot hors d'oeuvres made of cheese, bacon and olives on toothpicks, *pâté*—even caviar. And there was champagne, or the Prohibition simulation of it, to drink the health of the new book. We even rented an extra maid and a butler.

The party was in the afternoon. Berta Hader tells of arriving early and finding me sitting at the telephone, dressed in beige satin and lace hostess pajamas, rocking back and forth (I still have the little green rocking chair), tears streaming down my cheeks as I argued with the broker, who wanted more margin. We had been sending margin every day and were beginning to feel the hurt. These were our savings, our earnings—real money that we were withdrawing from the bank and dispatching to Wall Street. The broker was very gloomy. He hinted that it might be well for me to get out of the market. He said rather bluntly that he didn't think I could take it. About Stella, apparently, he had no such reservations. I felt that he was impugning my courage and so I valiantly assured him that I would stick just as long as Stella did. "Well . . ." he ended, and hung up, but it was obvious that he feared any minute to have me in violent hysterics on his hands and he had enough troubles without that.

In spite of my spurt of courage the conversation had depressed me greatly. For a little while Wall Street paper profits had obliterated my nightmare picture of a yawning poorhouse. With the paper profits dwindling, and my savings going after them, I was once again assailed by convictions of doom. The strange thing was that if I'd pulled out as the broker advised, I should still have had a tidy little sum of money. This I couldn't seem to realize. Apparently my idea—everybody's idea—was to save all or nothing.

Also, I was back at my old preoccupation of counting up costs. In my head I figured what all the little hors d'oeuvres, the butler, the maid, the near champagne, would set us back. I didn't see how we'd pay for it all. And then, suddenly, I remembered the Danish silver that had come into the country in bond. What would they do to me if I couldn't pay the duty? Arrest me, maybe. By that time I certainly was in no party mood. And when the other guests came, it seemed that all they could talk about was the stock market crash.

Stella had warned me that we must hide our predicament. She thought it bad business policy to seem pessimistic, since some of the guests were editors, and anyway she was never one to make a poor mouth. Besides, she said, it wouldn't be polite. If people knew they were eating our last caviar-smeared crusts they would be uncomfortable. All afternoon she watched carefully to make sure I wasn't saying anything I shouldn't.

Some of the guests besides Berta, however, saw through our masks of pretended gaiety. Julia Shawell told me months later that her heart nearly stopped beating when toward the end of the afternoon she walked into the room where guests had left their coats and found me leaning far out of a 16th story window, staring down at the street with desperation in my eyes. She tiptoed over and gently pulled me back from what she feared was a suicidal impulse. Of course I didn't know it then, but plenty of people were leaping out of windows that very day. She was wrong about me though.

The loss of money—even of my earnings along with the paper profits—would never have made me feel like suicide. Money as money was not that important to me, and it wasn't long after the party when it became evident that this was lucky because I was stripped absolutely bare. Every available cent I could lay my hands on had gone into the market and it wasn't enough, so all my stocks were sold. All of Stella's were sold too. We were completely broke, but before I handed over the dregs of my bank account I salvaged my Danish silver from the customs. Stella, staring at it morosely, said, "Well, maybe you can sell it."

I flared at that. "Indeed I won't sell it. I probably won't use it very much for a while but I'm going to keep it."

I did keep the silver but there was plenty else I had to give up. The rich advisor was no help now. He had too many difficulties of his own to worry about us.

One thing was immediately sure—we could no longer pay rent on the 16th-floor Park Avenue apartment. The renting company was very nice about it. They found me a cheaper apartment and said they would wait for the month I still owed and would even trust me for the first month's rent on the new place. I assured them that I was working on some stories that I would soon get paid for. Luckily, this was true. The depression didn't catch up with my magazine markets for a whole year, and 1930 from an earning point of view was one of the best I'd had since I started free-lancing. The trouble was that everything I took in had to go right out again.

The companies that held the mortgages on the house

I'd bought for my mother let me take advantage of the almost universal moratorium so that I neither had to pay the interest nor the amortization for a brief period. But how I did wish I had disregarded the advice of my rich advisor—now no longer rich—and paid for the house outright. I vowed, too, that if ever I got any money together again I'd buy an annuity. Except for these two regrets, I grieved only for my lost savings. They were what I thought of as real money. Besides, we were lucky. Stella still had her job and though I didn't expect it, 1930 was a really successful free-lancing year for me.

19. From Charm to Coolidge to Collapse

WHEN I called 1930 a "successful" year, I was thinking only about work and finances. Mentally, I relapsed into all my old anxieties and guilty fears, ending by celebrating New Year, 1931, by a complete nervous breakdown.

Neurologists are costly, so it was a good thing I had earned something like $40,000 in the previous 12 months.

231

The trouble was that after settling two mortgages and additional family obligations, paying back rent and the neurological fees, I was penniless again. Luckily the apartment I had taken after the crash was a bargain and having been poor so often, I can always manage.

Nineteen thirty began and ended with writing books. (I finished one right in the middle of the nervous breakdown.) When I first realized I could never turn out a great novel, I thought I didn't want to write books at all, but they kept coming my way and I had to keep on doing something.

One particularly I wish everybody could forget—including me. It was called *Charm*. Left to myself I'm sure I never would have attempted to tell anyone how to be charming. But I got a telephone call one day from Alexander Williams, a writer I'd known for a while, who had been collaborating on a book already commissioned by a publishing firm. The feminine co-author wanted to give up the collaboration and Sandy thought of me.

"The book needs a woman's touch," he declared, "and Rae Henkle [the publisher] is absolutely depending upon me to get it done. I promise to do most of the leg work if you'll just edit and revise."

I was appalled at the thought of letting my name be used in such a connection. I could just hear people saying, "Who does she think she is? Where does *she* get off to tell *me* how to be charming?"

However, Sandy was insistent, and I finally gave in. I can't remember how long it took, but not very long, I imagine, for I recall that a little French girl I knew said when she saw the published work: "Oh, I remember the day you wrote that!"

The book was dedicated to the Average American who,

according to Sandy and me, was almost as difficult to define as charm itself. Inevitably we quoted Sir James Barrie's line about that elusive quality from *What Every Woman Knows:* "If you have it, you don't need to have anything else. If you don't have it, it doesn't matter what else you have."

I find in looking over the book (probably the only copy in existence) that our Introduction credits the publisher as saying modestly that ours was a work which would "bring hope to the hopeless; shed light into the darkness of the unattractive."

Charm was issued on schedule but I had to take out my satisfaction in the pretty black and gold jacket, for I never got any royalties and the book has hounded me through the years. I go somewhere to make a speech and unless I forbid it beforehand, the introducer is more likely than not to mention archly that I once wrote a book on charm.

One thing I did learn from this venture—to be a little more careful about inscriptions that you put into books for friends and acquaintances. It seemed the most natural thing in the world to write *To ——— ———, the most charming person I know*. This worked fine until a few of my charming people began reading one another's inscriptions.

Alex Gumberg, an old friend, got me my next book assignment because he said he'd studied the field when I was on a New York newspaper and considered that I was by far the most efficient sob sister of the lot. That was a compliment so doubtful and even repugnant to me that I almost refused the commission, which was to write a human interest life story of Dwight W. Morrow, who was going to run for United States Senator from New Jersey.

At that time Mr. Morrow was known chiefly as a partner in the House of Morgan and Alex, his friend, felt he needed my "sentimental approach" and persuaded Dick Scandrett, Morrow's nephew, to agree with him.

I am sure that Mr. Morrow would have disapproved of the whole idea except that at the time he was in London as President Hoover's delegate to the Naval Disarmament Conference and never heard of the plan until it was too late to put a stop to it.

In fact, I had gathered most of the material before I ever met Mr. Morrow, which, as it turned out, was just as well since I didn't get much from him. He was interested in what he was doing—but the idea of a book about himself didn't have any allure for him.

He never knew, of course, how much he came to mean to me. Dwight Morrow was the first really great man with whom I came in contact—and one of the few in my whole life. Today he is probably best remembered by the world as the father-in-law of Charles Lindbergh. But to me he continues to be a hero on his own.

More than anybody I have ever known, he really cared about the public service jobs he was doing, not for the prestige they gave him, not for the sense of power, but for what they meant to the people for whom he did them.

A judge told me that Dwight Morrow was the greatest arbitrator in the world because it really mattered to him that disputants should agree for their best good.

In the absence of Mr. Morrow, I talked to Mrs. Morrow and her daughters at their home in Englewood, New Jersey, and liked them. There was an added interest to gathering material about Mr. Morrow because at the Morrow house the door would sometimes fly open and in would rush a tall, tousle-haired young man just back from somewhere and on his way somewhere else.

Mrs. Morrow would explain with a rueful smile,

"Charles [meaning her son-in-law Charles Lindbergh] is always on the go."

One day Elizabeth Morrow brought down to the luncheon table her nephew, the blond, blue-eyed Charles Lindbergh Jr. In the dreadful days of the world-wide search for him after he was kidnaped, I often remembered the smiling picture he made in the arms of his doting aunt whom he somewhat resembled.

The late Calvin Coolidge was Dwight Morrow's classmate at Amherst and the Morrow children were all fond of Coolidge stories that had been told them by their father.

During his year in Amherst, Morrow paid $3.50 a week for a room and three meals a day. Coolidge was a fellow boarder. There was a big black cat in the house which sometimes prowled around in the dining room, rubbing himself against the legs of the diners. Serving the boys was a waiter named Tibbetts, nicknamed Bitts. One night, after a long succession of the same, the chief dish at dinner was hash. Coolidge, served with his portion, inspected it for a moment and then called, "Bitts, bring me the cat."

Bitts, looking puzzled, went out and with some difficulty captured the animal. He returned with it spitting and clawing in his arms, held it out to Calvin Coolidge who looked at it for a long time, then ate his hash.

When Coolidge succeeded to the Presidency, his former classmates were approached for anecdotes about Amherst days. The Morrows brought out the pictures of the class of '95 and discovered that Coolidge, in the senior picture, was leaning against the very same post and in precisely the same position as in his freshman year.

Morrow was one of the first to suggest that in his former

classmate Massachusetts had material for the Presidency. He went to Amhert from the Republican Convention in Chicago the day after Coolidge was nominated for the Vice-Presidency and hearing that his friend was in Northampton, decided to call on him.

Coolidge himself opened the door of his half of the two-family house in which he then lived. He held in his hand a book on American history that he had been reading. Although his picture was on the front page of every paper that morning, there were no newspapers in the house.

"People are talking about you this morning, Calvin," said Morrow.

"Are they?" drawled Coolidge, dryly disinterested. "Well, by tomorrow they'll have found something else to talk about."

I too rang the Coolidge's doorbell in Northampton, but of a different house and a good many years later. My errand was to see Mrs. Coolidge about an article I was writing. Mr. Coolidge was ex-President then and died 10 days afterward. I think I was about the last reporter who ever talked to him and I wish I'd asked him something momentous.

I had written to Mrs. Coolidge asking for an appointment and received a very gracious refusal. A hunch told me that if I turned up in Northampton I might get my interview. So I boarded a train and from a hotel sent a note by messenger saying I was there and would she please see me for just a few minutes? Right away the telephone rang and a pleasant voice said, "This is Grace Coolidge and I'm sending the car for you."

She received me in her big comfortable living room. There was a bright fire burning in the fireplace and Mrs.

Coolidge knitted as we talked. After a while Mr. Coolidge came in. His wife introduced us and then went out of the room to see about getting the car to take me back to the hotel. Mr. Coolidge smiled and said, "I notice you came up after all."

"Yes, sir," I answered, "I did. It was so important to me to talk to Mrs. Coolidge that I took a chance and came."

"Well," he admitted, "that's the way. That's the way to get things. I'm glad you could come. My wife and I felt that we didn't want to embarrass the Administration at Washington by being in the limelight and that's why we've made the rule about interviews."

I mentioned that I had been in Washington the week before during a blizzard. He looked out the window and I, following the direction of his glance, saw that it was snowing heavily.

"Maybe you carry blizzards about with you," Mr. Coolidge suggested.

As I drove away, Mrs. Coolidge was waving and the ex-President was nodding and smiling. That's the way I see the 30th President of the United States every time I hear one of those jokes about unsociable, laconic Cal.

I wish I had the fascinating array of Presidential anecdotes that my friend Bess Furman does. She worked in the Washington Bureau of the Associated Press for years and now covers the capitol city for *The New York Times*. Bess was actually bitten by Meggie, predecessor to Fala as chief White House dog during the Roosevelt Administration.

Mrs. Roosevelt had given Bess a lift in her car and the dog, sitting between them, slashed Bess's lip. Mrs. Roosevelt drove the reporter at once to a hospital, then called the AP with an offer to write Bess's story. Some idiot in the bureau said politely, "Oh, no, Mrs. Roosevelt, we wouldn't think of putting you to so much trouble," thus doing his organization out of a contribution that would have been unique. For never before nor since has a President's wife substituted for a reporter who has just been bitten by a Presidential dog.

It would make a better story for me if Herbert Hoover had been President instead of Secretary of Commerce when I pushed him into an elevator that time. I wanted him to go up to the roof of the building which housed the American Child Health Association to have his picture taken. He protested that he had an appointment, but I was doing publicity for the association and that picture in *The New York Times* seemed to me much more important than any appointment the Secretary of Commerce could possibly have had.

Either he was a very forgiving man or else he forgot that it was I who propelled him into the elevator, for later when as President Mr. Hoover called the White House Conference on Child Health and Protection in Washington, he made no objection when Aida Breckinridge proposed that I handle the promotion.

That was a real job because the 1,200 experts on child care and protection throughout the country sent in voluminous reports together with recommendations. My job before the conference was to try to discover what it was all about—not easy, because they had their own social service vocabulary. After that I was supposed to boil down their findings into language the layman could understand and pass them out to reporters—when, of course, I could persuade the reporters to hold still for it.

I went to Washington four weeks ahead with Hilda Deichler—my wonderful secretary for many years—Helen Josephy, and a staff of bright young things, one at least so pretty that I figured she might be used to win over male recalcitrants among the press.

We were given a tiny cubicle in the Interior Department so that I could be supervised by Secretary of the Interior, Dr. Ray Lyman Wilbur, in charge of the conference.

Bess Furman, whom I met for the first time and liked on sight because she looked so honest and had my favorite color of hair—red—understood all the political undercurrents of the conference. I didn't and I didn't want to. I just wanted the conference to inaugurate a vast revolution in the care of children. I even dreamed that in a few years all boys and girls would be sound of mind and body.

I knew I had suffered in growing up from the lack of what the experts were beginning to call psychiatric help. It seemed to me that many of my problems as an adult— my perpetual uncertainty, my passion to be approved of at any cost—were hangovers from experiences in my childhood. I suspected I might have turned out differently if my mother could have had help.

The reporters were more interested in the political side of the convention—arguments and disagreements— than they were in plans for the children of the world. This discouraged me but I made the best of it by assigning my young scouts to cover the discord for the reporters, and in the process we were able to get in some telling blows for our side as well. Furthermore, our frankness won over some of the newspaper people so that they too became more or less passionate proponents for the cause of child health and protection. Foremost among these was Bess,

239

who had persuaded her desk to assign her not only to the conference for its duration but for the entire month before.

The day before the close of the conference, one of the staff brought word that the leaders had been called to a meeting at which Secretary Wilbur would bring them a secret message from the President about the final recommendations.

Secret meant no reporters. I wasn't invited either.

According to Bess, I am the one who suggested that we go over just before the meeting and inspect the reception room of the D. A. R. president-general's quarters where the gathering was to be held. We discovered a fine big coat closet in the room and just happened to be looking around inside it when the conference leaders started coming in. So of course we had to stay where we were.

Bess says that my anguished breathing could have been heard by the delegates if they had not been so intent on Dr. Wilbur's words. We heard Dr. Wilbur's talk and after the delegates finally straggled out, we went to my hotel to spend the next sixteen hours drafting and redrafting what we wished might be the conference findings, a document with teeth. Our frantic efforts were to no avail and we felt miserably that the final recommendations were inadequate. I think now that we expected too much, and nearly 30 years later I can see all sorts of benefits, all sorts of doors opened and opening as a result of Herbert Hoover's first White House Conference on Child Health and Protection. I'm glad I was part of it.

The book I finished in the middle of a nervous breakdown (the breakdown came on the heels of the White House Conference) was *New York Is Everybody's Town*, the last in a series of travel books that I did with Helen

Josephy. In the course of her work on the Paris *Herald*, Helen had collected an enormous amount of material about Paris—enough, she thought, for a book. But since she'd never written one, she was a little fearful about it. I seemed a veteran in her eyes, so she suggested that we work together.

Paris Is a Woman's Town, the result of this idea of hers, actually became a best-seller and led to *London Is a Man's Town* and *Beer and Skittles: A Friendly Guide to Modern Germany*, which fell upon evil days because it came out just when Hitler was growing powerful.

Up to the years of the publication of *New York Is Everybody's Town* there had been no New York City guides of the kind. But that fall at least six others emerged. Which seems to be what happens once anybody breathes an idea into the air. Editors have told me, in fact, that after they contract for a book on a brand-new subject, they are likely to get a flood of manuscripts from unrelated authors that seem almost like duplicates.

The fate of *New York Is Everybody's Town* was a sort of forerunner of what the next three years were to bring: many downs and very few ups!

20. *I Knew It Couldn't Last*

WHILE the years between 1930 and 1934 were certainly the most difficult of my life, I'm glad I had them. From being a moderate success as a newspaper and magazine writer, from having a reasonable amount of money to spend, from summers in Europe and a Park Avenue apartment with maid, I was suddenly plunged into complete poverty. Beginning all over again is tough when you have lost considerable of your youth and excitement about life. Besides, I was carrying heavy responsibilities.

Luckily I hadn't experienced luxury long enough to get accustomed to it. I'd had that feeling of unreality all the time I was living high, and an underlying conviction that it was too good to last and not right anyway. So being without money and having to start over again was not such a great shock to me. Perhaps it would have been harder if almost everybody I knew hadn't been in the same predicament. The more friends on the same mission I met on my job-seeking rounds, the more cheerful I felt, the easier my lot seemed.

I remember saying about this time, "If I could only be sure of $50 a week for the rest of my life, I wouldn't have a care in the world." This wouldn't have been true, for even with enough money to go on with I would always have been sunk about work. My inability to do it as well as I wished to do it has always been the really great cross of my life.

The magazine crash, when it finally came at the beginning of 1931, was as relentless and complete as the stock market debacle. Quite suddenly all the editors who had been my bread and butter were not buying anything. Their magazines each month were almost as thin as pamphlets. The few articles they did run came out of the safe —pieces that had been bought and paid for but for some reason never used. They were cutting down on staff, too, but if they had any assignments, the staff members still remaining got them.

I kept on sending ideas and outlines to Carol Hill, my agent, but I grew accustomed to getting them back. So since there evidently weren't going to be any magazine assignments, I started thinking about newspapers again.

One night when I was dining with my friends Mary

and Lem Parton, I got to talking about some old notes I'd come across that day. They were about a young woman I met who was from Missouri and had a background a good deal like my own—born on a farm, baptized at an early age into the Baptist Church, ambitious, like me, she had come to New York to make her fortune. But she had started out as a social worker, not a reporter, and at a friend's house had met a tall, good-looking young man with whom she instantly fell in love. He reciprocated and two months later they were married.

She assumed from what he said that he was in the real estate business, but after a honeymoon in Canada and three weeks in a little Long Island dream house, one of his associates blurted out the truth: her Prince Charming was a bootlegger. When I met her she was soon to have a baby and she was so torn with remorse and anxiety that before either of us knew it she was telling me the whole story.

Lem, who had an interest in a newspaper syndicate, said, "You've got a syndicated feature there. Why don't you write it? I think I can do something with it."

All evening we talked about Elsie and her experiences. They had been difficult for a naïve Missouri girl, as when one night an apprentice bootlegger was brought to her house, shot close to the heart, and out of his head. In his delirium he kept murmuring the name Lillian, and the enterprising Elsie found in his wallet the address of a Lillian and promptly telegraphed her. Lillian turned up two days later, and the two women between them persuaded the young man to give up bootlegging forever.

Elsie had been not without humor. She could still laugh, if grimly, at herself and sometimes at the situation. She lived in a section of Long Island where there were big estates and some of the caretakers were part of the bootleg gang, particularly useful when it came to storing booze brought in from Rum Row. On one occasion, the millionaire owner of an estate returned home unexpectedly to find his bathroom piled high with cases. He calmly appropriated the liquor, which happened to be of fine quality (it was still uncut) and immediately posted his property with signs reading NO TRESPASSING—EXCEPT IN UNUSUAL CASES.

She told, too, of a rich woman who raised prize poultry for a hobby and was inspecting her hen houses one morning when she found her hens flapping and floundering around the yard. She thought they had been stricken with some dreadful disease and summoned a veterinarian who dosed them for pips, the gapes and croup. They recovered and in the meantime she learned they were drunk. An enterprising rooster had pecked the cork out of a contraband bottle stored in the brooder, spilled the contents and the hen house had become the scene of a bender.

"You know," Elsie told me mournfully, "Ben was partly on business in Canada when I thought we were just on our honeymoon."

The last I heard of the young woman she had made up her mind to go home to Missouri to have the baby and was planning not to come back. She felt she just couldn't bear any longer the suspense and feeling of guilt.

Lem didn't like that for an ending. "Oh, no," he urged. "Have her go home to have the baby, think it all over and decide that her place is with her husband, no matter what his occupation. Besides, you can have her philosophize about how Prohibition is bound to end sometime and then Ben will be forced to become an honest man."

I thought that was a very masculine point of view and

registered a dissenting vote, but I needed the money. I eventually wrote 12 chapters of what we called "The Story of a Bootlegger's Wife, as told to Mary Margaret McBride." Time had somewhat dimmed my memory and I never have been able to read my own notes very well, so Elsie, the bootlegger's wife, echoed many of my own scruples and sentiments, particularly about liquor. I used to wonder if Elsie ever read the series, which was carried widely through the country. And I wish I could know how she came out. I hope the baby was a boy. Girls have a harder time than boys and being a bootlegger's daughter would be a handicap to her.

A lot of us have forgotten it now, but Elsie's experience wasn't so very unusual. Bootleggers weren't all racketeers and mobsters. A good many respectable citizens got sucked into the business in various capacities, partly to make money and partly because there was a general conviction that Prohibition violated the tenets of freedom upon which our country was founded. This was the alibi, at least, which Ben and his associates used on Elsie and others of their circle who had scruples.

Like Lem, friends who knew of my difficulties were constantly though sometimes apologetically coming to me with job suggestions. Apologetically because most of the jobs were temporary and very poorly paid. One woman told me about a magazine of the home and garden type that needed some garden articles rewritten. The magazine belonged to a publishing group for which I had often done pieces that my canny agent had sold for $1,500 and $2,000.

I went to see the garden editor, who asked me quite sharp questions about my gardening experience. He didn't seem particularly impressed with my years of writing, either. Finally he handed me a small manuscript which he looked at disparagingly.

"This is the worst written article we've ever had," he declared. "She has her facts right, but that's all. If you can make a readable article of it, we'll pay you $21. Then, if you do that all right, we might be able to throw some other things your way."

I thought sadly of the $2,000 check that I'd had less than a year before from one of the more important magazines of his group for a story not much longer than this. All the same, I worked as hard as I'd ever worked at anything, writing and rewriting the techniques of growing iris. I delivered the finished effort myself but the editor sent out word that he was too busy to see me and I was to leave the article with the receptionist. I did, and from that day to this I've never heard anything from it. I couldn't afford to buy the magazine to see whether they ran my rewrite and anyway I didn't want to know.

In the three and a half years of my private depression my clothes got shabby and my confidence in myself followed suit. Unfortunately, in my prosperous period I hadn't cared enough to accumulate a wardrobe that would have come in handy during the constant job hunting and I found that you are much more conscious of clothes when you don't know exactly where your next month's rent is coming from, more conscious too of the way prospective employers eye you from head to foot not missing a single shiny spot, ragged cuff or much-mended shoe. Stockings were the worst, for they would get runs—this was B.N. (Before Nylon)—and they were expensive.

I got so desperate one day that I wrote a rich cousin and flatly asked for a loan of $5,000. He sent it to me by the next mail. I never touched a cent of the money—it was a matter of pride with me not to—just kept it as a backlog, but it certainly was a wonderful comfort in the frequent moments of strain.

I held off as long as I could, but when all other efforts failed, I was finally forced to try to get a publicity job. This is to me the worst possible way to make a living in the writing field. In the first place, you have to ask favors of your friends, truckle to people you don't even like, and after you get your story planted, ten chances to one some kind of crisis will wipe it out, or else some editor who hates press agents will eliminate the copy. Your employer doesn't understand any of this and holds you responsible even for a revolution that kills the story about him. He is sure he is front-page material and can't understand why you don't get him there.

However, I had wonderful luck with my first depression publicity job. A mutual friend heard Margaret Bourke-White say that she wanted somebody to do a special piece of promotion for her. She was already a famous photographer, but she was interested in photographic murals which at the time were a new art idea. The friend recommended me to Margaret and thus began one of the most fascinating associations I ever had. Because I'd worked with Helen Josephy on the White House conference publicity job I called her in again and together, if I say it as shouldn't, we blanketed the country with stories about Margaret Bourke-White.

She was sure-fire copy (even in her college days she was a herpetologist) and best of all she allowed us to give away scores of her magnificent pictures. Furthermore, we never asked her to do anything that she didn't agree to with enormous cheerfulness, and sometimes she even went further than our suggestions. I can still feel a chill up and down my spine thinking of her on a windy morning poised on a narrow ledge beside a gargoyle forty-odd stories up on the outside of the Chrysler Building. Some photographer wanted a shot of her up there to illustrate one of our yarns.

I still have the wonderful letter Margaret Bourke-White wrote at the conclusion of our campaign. It should have been a great help in getting other jobs of the kind but there just weren't any. Helen and I went from office to office, united by fear and our need for money.

Helen had been studying yogi and we had taken, and probably edited slightly, certain bits of yogi wisdom which we repeated softly to ourselves just before we entered the office of a prospective employer. "I am a center of power and influence," we mouthed with as much confidence as we could churn up. "I can do all things and do them perfectly."

Probably the optimistic words took us through the interviews with less agony than we would otherwise have felt, but we seldom got the jobs. Toward the end of this excruciating period I actually had lines out for twenty-seven different situations in every area of communication except radio. I never even thought of that, for in the first place I never listened to it and in the second, never dreamed that I had any of the capabilities it could use.

Though it seemed quite sad to me at the time, one of the twists of fate right in here provided me with a story that has since enlivened many a dinner table and for that matter, many a dull speech I've made.

A friend, Barbara Johnson, got an idea for a series of little paper-covered biographies of motion picture stars to be sold in the five-and-ten-cent stores. She was so keen on the scheme that she asked me to go to Hollywood and try to get the stories. She would pay all expenses and if the plan succeeded, I stood to make a tidy sum. Since I wasn't doing much else, I agreed to go.

I flew to the Coast, carrying as a going-away present from a friend what she called a Hollywood nightgown, the flimsiest, most diaphanous garment I'd ever seen. I'd also made a last-minute purchase of two dresses which needed minor alterations, to be done by a California representative of the firm I'd bought the garments from.

Nothing in Hollywood went according to schedule. The movie stars, instead of being enchanted to be interviewed, balked. And, although no one in California called it that, rain fell and fell.

One particular afternoon I'd come in tired, discouraged and wet. All I wanted was to climb into a warm, dry bed, read an escape novel and eat milk toast for supper.

But the promised dressmaker was waiting for me. I reluctantly submitted as she turned me this way and that, stuck pins in me and chattered. Finally she left and with a luxurious sigh I arrayed myself in my Hollywood nightgown and dropped gratefully onto my bed. Then the telephone rang. It was the dressmaker. She'd left her rubbers outside my door and would I please take them inside and keep them until she could stop by?

Rather irritably, just as I was (and you mustn't forget my Junoesque proportions in a nightgown which left nothing to the imagination), I opened the door and noted the rubbers had been kicked down the hall a piece. Flinging the door wide, I glanced up and down the empty corridor and then stepped into the hall to retrieve the rubbers.

Well, a wind blew then and the door slammed behind me. I really think I went berserk. I beat on the door, crying piteously, "Let me in!" Then I turned and put on the rubbers. They were open-toed (I suppose only in California can you get open-toed rubbers) but I felt better in them, more poised, less undressed.

With the rubbers on, my reason also started to return. I looked up and down the corridor. There wasn't a soul in sight, but I thought there surely ought to be a maid somewhere, so I called, "Maid! Maid!"

I was near a stairway and a voice from the next floor replied, "What do you want?"

I cried, "I want to be let into my room!"

But there was no answer: there was never any answer.

Then I thought of the elevator. I could go around and ring the bell. Just as I started in that direction I saw in my mind's eye the smart-aleck elevator boy with his cap impudently tipped over one eye and the openwork elevator filled with passengers, all staring at me in my Hollywood nightgown.

Finally, I did the only thing I could do: looked for a slit of light under a door. I found one, across the way from my own room, and ran over to ring the bell peal after peal, calling, "If you're a man, don't open the door!" It opened instantly and a middle-aged woman gazed at me in amazement. I stammered out my plight. She whooped with laughter and drew me inside where a friend also found me very funny.

The women had come from the Midwest to Hollywood for a look at the wild goings-on they'd read about—and I'm certain that for a mad moment they thought they had found some. But they summoned a maid and I scuttled back to the sanctuary of my room.

The next night I was invited out to dinner. Sadly I told the man on my right of my terrible misadventure. Soon the whole table was in an uproar and after that I was invited out every night to tell the nightgown story. Moreover, it opened all the doors that had been barred to me. I interviewed Robert Montgomery, Irene Dunne, Marlene Dietrich, Joan Crawford, Clark Gable and a raft of others—everyone I'd been sent to get. But although I wrote my pieces, the little books just never sold well, and all I ever got out of it was the trip, the nightgown, and the story.

The first real break in the hard years came with a telephone call from Julia Blanshard, an old friend who was then woman's page editor of Newspaper Enterprise Association, a subsidiary of Scripps-Howard. Julia had been sick for some time and I think she must have heard about my troubles from people who knew us both. She said she was about to go into the hospital for an operation and she wanted somebody she could trust to give it back to her to take over her job until she was well enough.

I hurried immediately to see Fred Ferguson, president of NEA, and was then and there hired as a part-time temporary replacement for Julia. It was almost worth having had all the anguish just to be suddenly a salaried person again. Not that I was tempted to any flights of extravagance. The whole experience of the crash, the national depression and my own private one had made me very wary. Almost the best day I had in the three and a half years was the one when President Roosevelt closed all the banks, and I'm sure I was not alone in this. The whole country seemed to come out of its gloom long enough to go on a joyous personal bender. Nobody had any cash, everybody was suddenly willing to trust everybody else. It was lovely and I think most of us never afterwards sank so deeply into despair.

I was hired for part time at NEA but I gladly put in not only full time but overtime. I decided then that the ideal way of life for me was to have a city editor and a certain sum of money coming in at the end of every week. That way I felt a kind of peace and security.

Then right away, as so often happens when you get a break after you have been desperate, came the chance that brought me the biggest opportunity and the greatest happiness I've ever known.

I was asked to do a radio audition and—I got the job! But that's **another story.**